PERGAMON OXFORD SPANISH SERIES

General Editors: PROFESSOR R. B. TATE, PROFESSOR G. W. RIBBANS

The Spanish Traditional Lyric

The Spanish Traditional Lyric

EDITED BY

JOHN G. CUMMINS

Senior Lecturer in Spanish, University of Aberdeen

PERGAMON PRESS

Oxford · New York · Toronto · Sydney · Paris · Frankfurt

U.K.	Pergamon Press Ltd., Headington Hill Hall, Oxford OX3 0BW, England
U.S.A.	Pergamon Press Inc., Maxwell House, Fairview Park, Elmsford, New York 10523, U.S.A.
CANADA	Pergamon of Canada Ltd., 75 The East Mall, Toronto, Ontario, Canada
AUSTRALIA	Pergamon Press (Aust.) Pty. Ltd., 19a Boundary Street, Rushcutters Bay, N.S.W. 2011, Australia
FRANCE	Pergamon Press SARL, 24 rue des Ecoles, 75240 Paris, Cedex 05, France
WEST GERMANY	Pergamon Press GmbH, 6242 Kronberg/Taunus, Pferdstrasse 1, Frankfurt-am-Main, West Germany

To Elaine

Si me preguntaren
cuia soi, cuia,
de hun estudiante
d'Estremadura.

Foulché-Delbosc, 'Séguedilles', No. 19.

Contents

PART I 41

Acknowledgements

I wish to express my thanks to Dr. Pamela Bacarisse and Dr. Ian
Macdonald of the Department of Spanish, University of Aberdeen: to
the first for her help in interpreting certain Portuguese and *gallego*
poems, and to the second for his patient elucidation of the orthography
and meaning of Arabic material. I am also greatly indebted to Dr.
Richard Hitchcock, of the Department of Spanish, University of Exeter,
for advice concerning the texts of the *kharjas*, and to Mr. William
Johnstone, Senior Lecturer in Hebrew, University of Aberdeen, for his
invaluable assistance with the translation of the Arabic *muwashshaḥa*
of Part II, Section A. My task of preparing the typescript was greatly
eased by the reliability and willingness of Mrs. Margaret Garvie,
Secretary of the Department of Spanish, University of Aberdeen.

I am grateful to the New Directions Publishing Corporation, New
York, for permission to reprint four poems by García Lorca and an
extract from *Bodas de sangre* (see footnote 5, p. 167). Every effort has
been made to clear copyright in respect of four lyrics by Rafael Alberti
included in Part II, but it has not been possible to obtain a reply
from Sr. Alberti, whose silence has been taken as indicating
acquiescence.

Introduction

Poesía popular or poesia tradicional?

The verse contained in Part I of this anthology is representative of a
current which is present in the culture of the Peninsula from the earliest
medieval manifestations of vernacular literature to the present day. It is
popular in the sense that its fundamental and continuing function
throughout the millennium in which its existence is documented has been
the entertainment of the rural lower class. At certain periods, however,
the swing of literary fashion has brought such poetry to the attention
of a public more literate and more courtly, and has caused it to be
imitated by the poets catering for such a public, whose poems are in
some cases indistinguishable in form, theme and style from the lyrics
which they consciously emulate. Examples of the work of such poets are
included in Part I alongside anonymous popular material. The term
poesía popular, therefore, is inadequate as a description of a type of
verse whose tradition, while unbroken at the popular level, at times
embraces wider social and literary strata; in recent years, therefore, the
more inclusive term *poesía de tipo tradicional* has become more common.

The interest of the non-popular imitator or anthologist is in fact a
crucial element in the preservation of truly popular material, since the
popular tradition is only documented, and its contemporary
manifestations written down or published, at times when literate
attention is focused on it. It is, nevertheless, impossible to overstress
the importance of the Spanish peasant in the preservation of the lyric
tradition in the repeated periods when the pendulum of literary taste
swings away from it. Rafael Alberti has acknowledged this explicitly
and graciously: 'Mientras, la guardan los que siegan, los que recogen la
aceituna, los que cuidan las cabras, los que esperan, en fin, la posesión

1

de la tierra—y como éstos son campesinos de España, la aguardan, entre burlas y veras, cantando' (*La poesía popular en la lírica española contemporánea*, Jena–Leipzig, 1933, p. 20).

'. . . entre burlas y veras, cantando.' The traditional lyric is basically a sung poetry. The relatively conservative character of Spanish rural society has enabled such folk-song to survive in Spain in a much more lively state than the literature of other rural cultures, so that field-work can still add to our knowledge of the tradition, revealing startling links between the lyrics current today and those preserved in published or written form from earlier periods. The rural culture of which the lyric is a part is disappearing at a constantly accelerating rate, undermined by various modern phenomena: the change from an agricultural to an industrial economy; the emigration of young workers to the towns or to other countries; improved communications; the pressure of central, national standards on local procedures, modes of dress and forms of speech; the tempting, easily assimilable entertainments of cinema, radio and television, windows on a bright, alluring world of smartness and leisure. There are many villages in Spain now populated largely by old people and cripples; many already populated by no one, stifled by afforestation or drowned by reservoirs. When a village dies, its songs die with it. If future generations of literary *aficionados* choose to revive again the themes and forms of the traditional lyric, they will do so as scholarly investigators of a dead genre, and not, like their many predecessors, as temporary dabblers in a lively river of tradition. Like the ox-plough and the drove-road, the traditional lyric survives while it has a function. In the entertainment of country people, which has always been the lyric's basic function, it is being supplanted. It has long been an essential part of life for a people in particular circumstances, but these circumstances, after remaining in essence unchanged for hundreds of years, are now disappearing in a few generations.

The lyric is not dead yet. It is still possible, in much of rural Spain, to sit around a fire with a family and a group of neighbours and to hear them sing songs whose origins are unknown and whose beauty in some cases is very great. It is possible to record their songs on paper or on tape; this book includes material collected in such circumstances. But to record is to fossilize. The fifteenth-century scribe, writing the words of a lyric in his manuscript; the sixteenth-century printer setting up the type of an anthology; the twentieth-century field-worker with his little talking box which the *abuelita* finds such fun; all these pour their amber over a lyric at a single point in space and time, and preserve it for ever unchanging. This is a negation of a basic characteristic of the traditional lyric, which is its inherent capacity for alteration.

Verbal and musical variation

The numerous collections of folk-lyrics published by modern field-workers such as Schindler and Torner have amplified our knowledge of a fact already apparent from older manuscript and printed sources: there is no single and authoritative version of an individual traditional song. Except when the temporary interest of an educationally superior public intervenes, a song is preserved in the mind and mouth of a people largely illiterate; it is spread geographically and handed down through the generations by oral transmission. A forgetful person may hand on a truncated or distorted version; a lively creative intelligence may improve or lengthen it. Clearly every lyric must have started somewhere, not by the spontaneous combustion vaguely envisaged by the German Romantics (and seen by them as producing a poetry naturally truer and purer than that of the sophisticated, literate poet), but by a single act of anonymous creativity. But a traditional lyric is never finished; if it lives long, it will change; if it spreads widely, it will exist in different contemporary versions; even within a single village, there will be arguments about exact wording or order of lines. This variability contributes greatly to the richness of the lyric. Some variants are of course happier than others; a pedestrian original may acquire beauty, but beauty may be destroyed. We can only judge any version on its merits; greater antiquity or nearness to the original, in addition to being normally difficult or impossible to assess, is not an indication of greater worth.

Just like the song of which it is a part, each variant owes its birth to a single creative act. This may be a deliberate attempt at improvement, an improvisation necessitated by forgetfulness, or even an unconscious mistake of omission or confusion with another song. Many variants die at birth, stifled by the conservatism and inertia of listeners or fellow singers familiar with the version previously existing. The success

of a variant depends in part on the personality and popularity of its
initiator and subsequent transmitters within the group or village.
Limitations of space preclude the inclusion in this book of every available
version of every composition. In the notes to the poems in Part I, I quote
some of the more interesting individual versions. The sample sets of
versions given below are intended to illustrate more fully the nature of
the lyric as a *poesía que vive en variantes*.

> *1a.*   Arrojóme la portuguesilla
> naranjillas de su naranjal;
> arrojómelas y arrojéselas,
> y volviómelas a arrojar.
>
> > Montehermoso, Cáceres (Torner, *Lírica*,
> > No. 37).

This may or may not be the version of the song nearest to the original
form, but its antiquity is attested by

> *1b.*   Pues allá va, amigos,
> una gran tonada
> que ahora ha cien años
> nueva se llamaba:
>
> Arrojóme la portuguesilla
> naranjillas del su naranjal;
> arrojómelas y arrojéselas,
> y volviómelas a arrojar.
>
> > Torres Villarroel, VIII, p. 339.

The widespread and enduring popularity of this song is due in part to
the charm of the image (the throwing of oranges as an overture of love
which is duly reciprocated), but also largely to its verbal delights: the
pace engendered by the chain effect of ll. 1–2 (*portuguesilla / naranjillas,
naranjillas / naranjal*) accelerates with the tongue-twisting complication of
ll. 3–4, where the grammatical subject switches to-and-fro, chased about
by the object pronoun in a threefold verbal variation. The importance
of ll. 1–2 is mainly thematic; their basic content is susceptible of

variation in expression. A significant affective role is played by the diminutive endings, and diminutives too are open to variation. The essence of the song, however, is the syntactical battle of ll. 3–4, to vary which would be to detract from its impact. In the following versions this tight and compressed kernel is generally preserved, whereas the more relaxed beginning is more open to alteration, though its varying diminutives keep it on a similar affective level.

In

> *1c.* Arrojóme las naranjicas
> con los ramos del blanco azahar;
> arrojómelas y arrojéselas
> y volviómelas a arrojar.
>
> *Tonos castellanos.*

and

> *1d.* Arrojóme las naranjuelas
> con los ramos del blanco azahar;
> arrojómelas y arrojéselas
> y volviómelas a arrojar.
>
> Lope de Vega (*Biblioteca de Autores Españoles*, Vol. XXXVIII, p. 256).

the girl becomes slightly depersonalized to make room for an additional symbolic element, the orange-blossom (carried in Spain by the bride). The same linking of symbols is also seen in a more relaxed and contemplative reworking of the song in

> *1e.* A una máscara salí
> y paréme a su ventana;
> amaneció su mañana
> y el sol en sus ojos vi.
> Naranjitas desde allí
> me tiró para favor;
> como no sabe de amor,

piensa que todo es burlar;
pues a fe que si se las tiro
que se le han de volver azâr.
Naranjitas me tira la niña
en Valencia por Navidad;
pues a fe que si se las tiro
que se le han de volver azâr.

Lope de Vega, *El bobo del colegio* (*Obras*,
2nd series, 13 vols., Madrid, 1916–30,
Vol. XI, p. 526).

In

1f. Arrojóme las mançanitas
por encima del mançanar;
arrojómelas y arrojéselas
y tornómelas a arrojar.

Luis de Briceño, *Método de guitarra*,
Paris, 1626.

the symbolic fruit is altered, but the *naranjillas* / *naranjal* pattern of *1a*
is preserved. This is lost, however, in the more rigorous parallelism of

1g. Arrojómelas i arrojéselas
por encima del mançanal;
arrojómelas i arrojéselas
i tornómelas a arrojar.

Foulché-Delbosc, 'Séguedilles', No. 332.

In a modern Aragonese version,

1h. Cogedme las manzanetillas
debajo del manzanetar;
cogédmelas y arrojádmelas
y volvédmelas a tirar.

Mingote, p. 16.

the tension evaporates with the abandonment of the double subject. Some of the various *culto* versions preserve the syntactical tension of the ending, e.g.

> *1i.* Arrojóme las perlas el Nenio
> por hacer a Moresco llorar;
> arrojómelas y arrojéselas
> e tornómelas arrojar.
>
> *Villancico morisco*, 1675 (Torner, *Lírica*, p. 86).

In others, however, it is relaxed:

> *1j.* Arrojóme el señor Cupidillo
> las saetas que flecha veloz;
> arrojómelas y arrojéselas
> y venimos a amar los dos.
>
> MS. 14,088 (1703).

or parodied:

> *1k.* Yo como la vi burlar,
> las manos le así y beséselas;
> y arruñómelas y arruñéselas
> y tornómelas a arruñar.
>
> Tirso de Molina, *Antona García* (*Nueva Biblioteca de Autores Españoles*, Vol. IV, Madrid, 1906, p. 620).

In many other examples of lyrics without refrain-repetition, it is common for the opening lines to be preserved as the kernel of the many versions, as in the examples *2a–2s*, below. This set, by no means exhaustive, exemplifies too the intricate web of formulae which can not only link different versions of the same lyric, but can also be used in the treatment of varying motifs at more than one emotional level.

2a. Al pasar el arroyo
     de Santa Clara,
     se me cayó el anillo
     dentro del agua.

>   Cuevas de Ágreda, Soria (Schindler,
>   No. 642).

2b. Al pasar el puente
     de Villamediana,
     se me cayó el pañuelo
     y me lo ha llevado el agua.

>   Castile (Torner, *Lírica*, p. 41).

2c. Al pasar del arroyo
     de Brañigales,
     me dijeron amores
     para engañarme.

>   Lope de Vega, *Al pasar del arroyo* (*Obras*,
>   2nd series, Vol. XI, p. 280).

2d. Al pasar del arroyo
     de Canillejas,
     vióme el caballero,
     antojos lleva.

>   Lope de Vega, *Al pasar del arroyo* (*Obras*,
>   2nd series, Vol. XI, p. 280).

2e. Al pasar de el aroio
     de el alamillo,
     las memorias de el alma
     se me an perdido.

>   Foulché-Delbosc, 'Séguedilles', No. 68.

In *2a–2e*, the durable element in both Golden Age and modern versions is l. 1; l. 2 is varied to suit different localities, and the main variation is in ll. 3–4; the tone of the five versions is similar. Compare, however,

2f. Al pasar el arroyo
de Las Perdices,
agarré un peludito[1]
de las narices.

Argentina (Magis, p. 490).

This preserves the pattern of *2a–2e*, but the tone of ll. 3–4 is now burlesque. This change must have been all the more effective when this variant was first introduced, because there must have been a general awareness of the normal tone of songs with the same beginning, and otherwise the change would have had little point. This contrast may now have lost its effectiveness in the local setting.

2g. Al saltar el arroyo
te vi los bajos;
yo creí que eran flecos
y eran colgajos.

Castile (Torner, *Lírica*, p. 49).

2h. Al saltar el arroyo
te vi los bajos;
yo pensé que eran flecos
y eran pingajos.

Rodríguez Marín, *Cantos*, No. 7117.

2i. Al pasar del aroio
le vi las piernas;
¡ai de putha bellaca,
qué blancas qu'eran!

Foulché-Delbosc, 'Séguedilles', No. 75.

2j. Al pasar del aroio
las piernas la vi;
que no valen un quarto
ni un maravedí.

Foulché-Delbosc, 'Séguedilles', No. 76.

[1] *Agarrar un peludo*, 'to get drunk'.

Versions *2g–2j* look at first like more sweeping parodies of the tradition of *2a–2e*, but they really represent a different thematic current, most of whose manifestations begin *Al saltar el arroyo*, as do *2g* and *2h*. Versions *2i* and *2j*, however, are contaminated by the wording of l. 1 of versions *2a–2e*.

> *2k.* Al pasar por tu puerta
>   te ví las ligas;
>   como eran de color
>   se espantó el burro.
>
> Diustes, Soria (Schindler, p. 31).

Version *2k* shows a further overlapping of traditions; the content and tone of ll. 2–4 are similar to those of *2g–2j*, but l. 1 is borrowed from a separate current again, whose content and tone are exemplified by

> *2l.* Al pasar frente a tu casa
>   me tiraste con un limón;
>   el limón cayó en el suelo
>   y el dolor fue en el corazón.
>
> Argentina (Magis, p. 456).

There are further parodies of the tradition of *2l*, e.g.

> *2m.* Ayer pasé por tu casa,
>   me tiraste un brasero;
>   si no paso tan ligero
>   me pegas en el trasero.
>
> Argentina (Magis, p. 284).

The chain can thus go on *ad infinitum*. An additional element of variation is the musical setting. The same or very similar words are often sung in different areas to tunes partly or completely different, and the varying musical treatments may necessitate alteration of the text by repetition or by exclamatory insertions. Thus *2a*, above, is sung in another province of Spain with a different tune and with two stanzas:

2n. Al pasar el arroyo
de Santa Clara,
se me cayó el anillo
dentro del agua.

Por coger el anillo
cogí un tesoro:
una Virgen de plata
y un Cristo de oro.

Anciles, León (Schindler, No. 399).

These same two stanzas are sung elsewhere to a tune necessitating line-repetition of different kinds:

2o. Al pasar el arroyo
de Santa Clara,
se me cayó el anillo
dentro del agua,
se me cayó el anillo
dentro del agua.

Por coger el anillo
cogí un tesoro,
con la Virgen de plata
y el Cristo de oro;
y el Cristo de oro
y el Cristo de oro,
y al pasar el arroyo
cogí un tesoro.

Santorcaz, Madrid (Schindler, No. 482).

A more regular pattern of repetition characterizes an extended version of the song used as an accompaniment to a children's game:

2p. Al pasar el arroyo
de los linares, } twice

me se ha perdido el libro⎫
de los cantares.   ⎬ twice

Al pasar el arroyo   ⎫
de la Victoria,   ⎬ twice

tropezó la madrina,   ⎫
cayó la novia.   ⎬ twice

La madrina se ríe,   ⎫
la novia llora,   ⎬ twice

porque se le ha manchado⎫
toda su joya.   ⎬ twice

Sarnago, Soria (Schindler, No. 824).

In two further versions, also used to accompany games, the tunes are
again different, and the song is filled out not only by repetition but also
by exclamatory insertions:

2q. Al pasar el arroyo,
        ¡ay, ay, ay!
        de Santa Clara,
        ¡dengue, dengue, dengue!
        de Santa Clara,
        ¡litón, litón, litón!

Sepúlveda, Segovia (Schindler, No. 538).

2r. Al pasar el puente
        de Santa Clara,
        ¡ay, ay, de Santa Clara!
        me se cayó el anillo
        dentro del agua,
        ¡ay, ay, dentro del agua!

Laina, Soria (Schindler, No. 690).

The song was expanded in a similar manner in the Golden Age, as we
see in a further version of *2e*:

2s. Al pasar del arroyo
del alamillo,
¡jum, jum!
las memorias del alma
se me han perdido,
¡jum, jum,
galandú, galandú!
las memorias del alma
se me han perdido.

Villanelle di più sorte (Torner, *Lírica*, p. 42).

In our third set of versions, below, as well as the mild variants in the wording of *3a–3c*, and the parodies of *3d–3f*, we have in *3g–3k* a series in which the durable kernel is the restricted but very expressive theme:

3a. Por la calle abajito
va quien más quiero;
no le veo la cara
con el sombrero.

Baile del rio i del barquillero, 1703 (Torner, *Lírica*, p. 403).

3b. Por la calle abajito
va quien yo quiero;
no se le ve la cara
con el sombrero.

La Mancha (Torner, *Lírica*, p. 402).

3c. Por la calle abajito
va quien yo quiero;
no le veo la cara
con el sombrero.

Mal haya en el sombrero
que tanto tapa;
yo le compraré uno
para las Pascuas.

Extremadura (Torner, *Lírica*, p. 402).

3d. Por la calle abaxito
va quien más quiero;
no le veo la cara
con los tacones.

Baile de los disparates, MS. 14,088.

3e. — Aquí tienes mi afecto,
¿qué le reparas?
— La cara no le veo
con las polainas.

Mojiganga de Roxillas, early seventeenth
century (Torner, *Lírica*, p. 403).

3f. Por la calle abajito
va mi comadre
con el abanico
dale que dale.

Argentina (Magis, p. 394).

3g. Mal haya la falda
de mi sombrero,
que me quita la vista
de quien bien quiero.

Correas, *Arte*.

3h. Yo no quiero el sombrero
de ala muy grande,
por si el ala me quita
ver tu semblante.

Murcia (Sevilla, p. 198).

3i.   Esa tu boina, majo,
tate bien, cálesla muncho;
lo moreno de tu cara
no lo puedo ver a gusto.

Asturias (Torner, *Lírica*, p. 402).

3j.   Álzate esa gorra, majo,
que no se te ven los ojos,
esos labios de coral
y ese moreno gracioso.

Castile (Alonso Cortés, p. 112).

3k.   Trazeis o chapeu baixinho,
mandae-o arredondar,
que debaixo d'elles andam
dois olhos a namorar.

Portugal (Torner, *Lírica*, p. 402).

Examples are given above (*2n–2s*) of the appearance of a lyric in different areas with different tunes. The opposite process is also common: a single tune may be used for different lyrics with a common form. This is particularly frequent in the case of the simpler four-line forms in the modern period, but also occurred earlier with other fixed forms such as the *zéjel* (see p. 23). The following is a simple modern example of the phenomenon, a group of thematically unrelated lyrics, composed separately, but collected by Schindler as a sequence, sung to a single tune:

Un soldado me dió un ramo,
yo lo cogí con cautela,
que en la mano del soldado
no puede haber cosa buena.

Gitanilla, gitanilla,
díme la buena ventura.
No te la puedo decir,
que no soy gitana pura.

La calle abajito baja
un ratón haciendo media,
las agujas son de palo
y el ovillo de madera.

Torreblancos, Soria (Schindler, p. 41).

In the case of lyrics with a refrain, involving an alternation of soloist and chorus, the overall communal awareness is centred on the refrain, which is therefore the part of the song most subject to restrictive conservatism. Consequently, in two different versions of a lyric, widely separated in time or space, the refrain may be the same, or largely so, whereas the solo stanzas may vary considerably. The link between a refrain and a tune is very durable, but the intervening stanzas may be newly composed at any time, and are sometimes lyrics which have had a separate previous existence. This marrying of words and tunes originally existing separately can happen in cases where the logical stress of the words and the musical stress of the tune do not coincide. Thus we have songs in which the logical stress is preserved in the refrain, linked with the tune from the outset, but dislocated in the solo stanzas, whose words were composed separately. In the following example the musical stress is marked with an accent, and it will be seen that this largely coincides with the logical stress in the chorus, but diverges markedly from it in the stanza:

No quieró que me quiéran,
ní ser queridá;
quiero sér de los hómbres
áborrecidá.

Chorus: Por el áire, pór el aire
ván los suspíros de mi amánte;
pór el aire ván, por el áire.

Asturias (Torner, *Cancionero*, No. 194).

All the versions of this song collected by Torner, with different stanzas and the same refrain, showed similar dislocation of stress in the stanza.

This application of a tune to any set of words with a suitable syllable-count may also explain the oddities of stress in some Golden Age examples, but this is not invariably the explanation. There is a certain freedom of stress in the lyric, and in cases such as the following the dislocation is already necessitated by the rhyme:

> Solía que andaba
> el mi molinó,
> mas agora no.
>
> Correas, Vocabulario.

> En la huerta nasce la rosa:
> quiérome ir allá
> por mirar al ruiseñor
> cómo cantabá.
>
> Gil Vicente, Auto dos Quatro Tempos
(Obras completas, Vol. I, p. 105)

The basic lyric, though its parts may change, may nevertheless be extremely durable. Many songs still in existence orally are very old, and some have changed remarkably little in a period of centuries. An important result of modern field-work has been the revelation of precise and striking links between lyrics whose existence is documented in the Golden Age and versions of the same lyrics existing in the twentieth-century oral tradition of rural Spain, South America and North Africa. Examples of such survivals may be found in the notes to individual lyrics in Part I.

The language of the lyric

Most of the lyrics in this anthology are in Castilian, now the standard language of Spain, but originally the dialect of a limited area of Central Northern Spain. The traditional lyric existed before Spain became unified and before Castilian became the standard language, and even now, since the lyric is basically popular and rural, it persists in areas where Castilian has not yet usurped the local dialect, which remains the linguistic vehicle in which the lyric exists.

When the invading Arabs occupied the central and southern areas
of the Peninsula in the eighth century, only a proportion of the Christian
population of the conquered Visigothic kingdom fled before them to the
north. Many of the romance-speaking Christians remained in areas
under Arab rule, maintaining their romance dialect. The oldest lyrics in
this collection, the *kharjas*,[2] are in a form of *mozárabe*, the dialect of these
people, though it is perhaps a little early, in the present state of
scholarship, completely to identify their language of communication
with that of the *kharjas*. The reasons for the survival of these ancient
lyrics are explained in Part II; briefly, they survive because courtly poets,
writing mainly in Arabic or Hebrew, took an interest in them and
incorporated them in their own verses.

The next-oldest poems in the book, as well as some more recent ones,
are in *gallego*, the dialect of Galicia. The vagaries of literary fashion in
the thirteenth and fourteenth centuries caused *gallego* to be used as the
language of lyric poetry in the Castilian court and noble households.
The effect of this is that the traditional lyrics surviving from this period
are written in *gallego*. In the case of both the *mozárabe* and the *gallego*
lyric, one must beware of supposing that, since the only traditional
lyric material surviving from a certain period is in one or the other
dialect, no popular lyric was in existence in Castile, León, or any other
area of Spain in the dialect of which no early material has survived.

In the late medieval period, Castilian comes to be used as the main
language of sophisticated lyric poetry, and in the early Golden Age,
coinciding with the spread of the printing press, there is an enormous
literary interest in the traditional lyric. A high proportion of the poems
in this book are taken from the Castilian *cancioneros* (anthologies of
verse, often though not invariably musical) and other collections of
the fifteenth century and early Golden Age. Examples not in Castilian
from this period are rare, though of course the lyric lived on,
undocumented, at the popular level in Galicia and other non-Castilian
areas.

In late years, field-workers have recorded large numbers of traditional
lyrics at the popular level, in both Castilian and non-Castilian areas.
Notable endeavours in this direction were Torner's investigations of the
songs of Asturias and Galicia (his *gallego* collections were destroyed,

[2] See Part II, Section A.

unpublished, in the Civil War), and Schindler's recording journeys through various provinces of Spain and Portugal. This anthology, then, while consisting mainly of Castilian texts, also includes lyrics in *mozárabe*, *gallego* and modern western dialects. The Catalan-speaking area is excluded. The vocabulary of non-Castilian examples may be found below the text concerned, and I have included explanatory notes wherever I have thought that the meaning of a lyric may be obscure to a reader acquainted only with Castilian.

Tradition in style and meaning

The traditional lyric is on the whole uncomplicated and presents few grammatical difficulties. Word-order is usually straightforward, and syntactical and metrical units (and the musical unit, in sung lyrics) almost invariably coincide. The habitual brevity of the lyric leaves no room for verbosity, and means that, if the tiny poem is to say anything very much, it must employ a language of association and allusion and so transcend its formal limitations. To understand the lyric fully, to see beyond its immediate charm on a superficial level, we must read more than just a few dozen poems; we must immerse ourselves sufficiently for an awareness of this language to become an almost subconscious part of our appreciative equipment, as it is from childhood for the oral preserver of the lyric.

Take for example the simple and commonplace phrase *mis ojos*. This occurs commonly in the lyric in the first line or two, and carries a weight of meaning out of proportion to its brevity ('my beloved, the thing I love and need most in this world, the means by which my perception of life is brightened and intensified, the loss of which would be intolerable agony . . .', etc.). The fact that this meaning is conveyed so briefly may allow us to pass over the phrase almost without registering it on first reading, for instance,

> En Ávila, mis ojos,
> dentro en Ávila (see Part I, No. 223),

but a more extensive familiarity with the lyric reveals that breadth of meaning is attained by allusion to a tradition both ancient and contemporary in which various literal and figurative usages of *ojos* conventionally evoke certain associations, as in these examples:

Ya nunca verán mis ojos
cosa que les dé placer
hasta volveros a ver.

> Pedro de Padilla, *Romancero*, Madrid, 1583.

¡Ay, ojuelos verdes;
ay, los mis ojuelos!
¡Ay, hagan los cielos
que de mí te acuerdes!

> C. *General*, 1557 (text from *Antología*, No. 163).

Ojuelos graciosos
que os estáis riendo
del que está muriendo.

Ojos tan hermosos,
doléos de min;
no me déis la fin,
basten mis enojos.
Miradme, mis ojos,
aunque sea riendo
del qu'está muriendo.

> *Cancionero de Elvas, ca.* 1540 (text from Alín, No. 293).

Por vida de mis ojos,
el caballero;
por vida de mis ojos
bien os quiero.

> Vásquez, *Recopilación*, II, 44.

Adiós, vida de mi vida;
tu vuelta, ¿quién la irá a ver?
Ya se van mis tristes ojos;
mi suerte, ¿cuál irá a ser?

Argentina (Magis, p. 386).

This, then, is another facet of the traditional nature of the lyric: we must be aware not only of the importance of tradition as an agent of preservation and variation, but also of the inseparable relationship of meaning between a single lyric and the tradition behind and around it. There are many phrases and motifs which, like *mis ojos*, carry a weight of traditional meaning.

Let us examine, for example,

Miraba la mar
la malcasada;
que miraba la mar,
cómo es ancha y larga.

MS. 3924, fol. 67.

Considered strictly within its formal limits, this is a success. Such syntactical straightforwardness and outward simplicity of statement are typical of the traditional lyric, often strengthening by contrast the complex emotions only hinted at by the wording. As a mere description of the sea, the poem achieves a good deal: the repetition of *miraba la mar*, and the insistent *m* of ll. 1–3 recreate in us the mesmeric effect of the sea on the girl; the meaning of the brief adjectives of l. 4 is reinforced by the persistent open *a* running through all four lines, and by the unfolding of horizons in the longer last line. There is an easy and effective movement from one tense to another, from objective description to subjective reaction.

The poem is raised from this pleasant but placid and largely visual level by the presence of the single word *malcasada*. We need no further details as to why the girl through whose eyes we are enabled to look is unhappy; this single discordant note is sufficient to transform our reactions to the description of the sea, to further subjectivize the reaction in l. 4, and to introduce tensions which belie the placidity of syntax,

statement and image. Substitute *morenita* for *malcasada* and the effect of
the poem, the implications of the power and mesmerism of the sea, and
the sea itself, almost, become shallower. So far we are still within the
poem's formal limits. But being traditional (and not simply conservative)
it can dispense with much, obtaining breadth by mere allusion to
elements of the tradition which precedes and surrounds it: to other seas
which separate lovers, attract suicides, provoke vaguely disturbing or
specifically sexual feelings (see Part I, Nos. 101–16); to other *malcasadas*
with more clearly specified problems (see Part I, Nos. 133–46). The
awareness of this common ground of tradition enabled an author
(possibly not the original author) to juxtapose the two elements in a new
and felicitous combination in which their traditional implications can
interplay and be thus heightened, without being formally stated.
Tradition is acting not as a restriction but as a liberator. I have tried to
explain the traditional associations of other thematic elements in the
introductions and notes to the various sections of Part I. In my
arrangement of poems in Part I, one of my more important aims has
been to show how stylistic and thematic elements over-ride linguistic,
geographical and chronological divisions.

The femininity of the lyric

A high percentage of the lyrics in this book express feminine emotions
and viewpoints. This is clearly the effect (and not the cause) of the simple
fact that the female members of a Spanish rural community sing more
than the men; singing is often a group activity, and the women are more
commonly gathered in a group in the execution of their daily activities,
washing clothes, spinning, sewing, etc., while the men's occupations,
except at certain seasons, tend to be more solitary. There are exceptions
to this: there are songs in each village normally sung as serenades to the
girls by the young men, some male work songs survive, and the male
singer is important in the *flamenco* song of Andalucía. The field-researcher,
however, can always collect more material from the women, and in any
social gathering of neighbours the verses of the songs will be sung by
one or other of the women, with the rest of the women, and sometimes
one or two of the more extrovert of the men, joining in the refrain.

The principal forms

The *zéjel* (< Arabic *zâǧil*, 'to sing'), though the number of stanzas may vary, has a fixed rhyme-scheme:

AA   bbbaAA   cccaAA   dddaAA   eeeaAA   ...   (AA = refrain).

The line-length varies. The earliest manifestations of this form are in Hispano-Arabic poetry, and defenders of the Arabist thesis have taken this as an indication that the form was invented by the Arabs and adopted later by Christian poets (notably in the thirteenth century by King Alfonso X, whose *Cantigas de Santa María* are mostly in *zéjel* form). It is possible, however, that the form was indigenous to the Peninsula: the system of refrain-repetition, unusual in classical Arabic verse, dominates Spanish popular verse, so that the *zéjel* form, which was almost certainly not brought to Spain by the Arabs, may have been adopted by them in imitation of processes they found there. The *zéjel*, common in medieval court verse, has some popularity in traditional verse of the late fifteenth and early sixteenth centuries (see Nos. 6, 135), but occurs only sporadically afterwards. Modern oral examples are extremely rare (see Torner, *Lírica*, pp. 415–17).

The *villancico* shows similarities to the *zéjel*. It consists of an introductory *estribillo* of two to four lines, which is developed in a series of longer stanzas, each of which ends with a return to the *estribillo*, repeating all or part of it. The many possible rhyme-schemes include:

ABB   cdcd   dbB
ABB   cddc   dBB
ABB   ccdd   AB

The line-length is usually six or eight syllables (for examples, see Nos. 4, 33, 99, etc.). The term *villancico*, originally designating only the *estribillo*, is applied in the Golden Age to the complete poem, and later is used commonly in the restricted sense of 'Christmas carol'.

There is some confusion of terminology between *villancico* and *glosa*. The *glosa* or gloss, in a narrow sense, is a poem with an initial theme which is amplified by a series of stanzas which comment on it and repeat its lines one by one, with successive lines of the theme forming the final line of each stanza. The *glosa*, in this restricted sense, is mainly a courtly rather than a traditional form. In those cases mentioned above, however, of poems in traditional *villancico* form in which the actual term *villancico* is applied exclusively to the *estribillo*, the *glosa* is the amplifying stanza or stanzas, and such a poem may be headed in the manuscript *Villancico con su glosa nueva*.

The *seguidilla*, in its basic form, is a stanza of four lines:

> a (six or seven syllables),
> b (five syllables),
> c (six or seven syllables),
> b (five syllables).

The rhyme in lines 2 and 4 is normally assonantal only (see Nos. 90, 91, etc.). This basic form is occasionally extended by three more lines:

> d (five syllables),
> e (seven syllables),
> d (five syllables),

and the number of syllables may fluctuate from seven to eight, or from five to six, although the alternation of longer and shorter lines is maintained. The *seguidilla* is, on available evidence, the longest-lived Spanish verse-form: it is found already in the Mozarabic *kharjas*, it is common in the Golden Age, and it persists in the twentieth century in folk-song and in the work of such poets as García Lorca and Alberti.

The other basic four-line form is the octosyllabic *copla*, usually rhyming, like the *seguidilla*, abcb (the rhyme again being assonantal only; see Nos. 107, 232).

The *cosaute* (mistakenly called *cosante* until recently) is a series of couplets separated by a short and invariable *estribillo* and, like the other forms with refrain, would normally involve delivery by a soloist and chorus:

> aaB   ccB   aaB   ccB   aaB   ccB   ...
> $\qquad\qquad$ (B = refrain; this is often a couplet BB)

(see p. 35 and Nos. 2, 16, 17, 29, etc.).

def. of seguidilla
def. of cosaute

The binary structure of the lyric

The basic nucleus of the lyric is commonly a balanced juxtaposition of two elements: an initial statement, followed by a grammatical and/or thematic extension of some kind. The extension may be an amplification of the initial statement, a reaction to it, or a reiteration or paraphrase of it. This binary pattern may be seen in many *estribillos*, with different numbers of lines, and also in the *seguidilla* and other four-line forms:

1   Este pradico verde,
2   trillémosle y hollémosle.

> *Silva de varios romances*, 1561 (text from Alín, No. 483).

1   ¡Qué bonica soys, hermana!
2   Bien pareçéys toledana.

> MS. 17,698, No. 25.

1   Aguas de la mar,
2   {miedo he
      que en vosotras moriré.

> Luis Milán, *El cortesano*, 1561 (text from Alín, No. 482).

1   {Que no puede navegar
      el marinero,
2   {que los ayres del amor
      se le han vuelto.

> MS. 17,698, No. 34.

1   {Porque me ven chiquita
      piensan que no sé querer;
2   {¡también las chiquitas saben
      amar y corresponder!

> Argentina (Magis, p. 505).

Reiteration and parallelism

Out of this basic binary pattern springs much of the rhythmic movement and musicality of the lyric, its preoccupation with repetition, insistence, echo; with phonetic, syntactical and conceptual parallelism. The results can vary from a largely unconscious use of sound-repetition to a formal parallelism of idea and syntax in which the resources of poetic expression themselves become the primary elements in the poem.

Repetition in vowel patterns

The innate musicality of many lyric texts is due largely to the delicacy and deftness of the vowel patterns, and in particular to the use of a recurring vowel or sequence of vowels. The *malcasada* poem quoted above (p. 21) is an extreme example of the importance of a recurring vowel, with the *a* occurring in all the stressed syllables and being echoed in many of the unstressed ones. There are many other cases of the anticipation of the stressed vowel of the line-ending by the same vowel in earlier stressed syllables:

> Si le mato, madre, a Juan,
> si le mato, matarme han.

> Francisco Salinas, *De Musica*, 1577 (text
> from Alín, No. 646).

> ¡Ay, amor, cómo soys puntoso!
> La darga dandeta.

> Francisco Salinas, *De Musica*, 1577 (text
> from Alín, No. 645).

A dominant vowel in one line may echo the vowel of the rhyme-word of the preceding line, or anticipate that of the following line:

> ¿Qué me queréis, caballero?
> Casada soy, marido tengo.

> *CMP*, No. 198.

Entra Mayo y sale Abril,
tan garridico le vi venir.

CMP, No. 76.

A step forward from this repetition of a single vowel is the repetition
of vowel sequences. At the end of the line, this may simply constitute
the assonantal rhyme which is normal in Spanish popular verse, but a
sequence of vowels may also recur internally, either within the same line:

Pinguele, respinguete,
¡qué buen San Juan es éste!

C. Colombina, fol. 86.

Niña y viña,
peral y habar,
malo es de guardar.

C. Colombina, fol. 72ᵛ.

or in stressed vowels of separate lines:

Rodrigo Martínes
a las ánsares, ¡ahé!,
pensando qu'eran vacas,
silvábalas, ¡hé!

CMP, No. 12.

or in parallel series of stressed and unstressed vowels in separate lines:

Por encima de la oliva
mirame el amor, mira.

MS. 3924, fol. 67ᵛ.

¡Sañosa está la niña!
¡Ay Dios! ¿quién le hablaría?

Gil Vicente, *Auto da Sibila Casandra* (see
Part I, No. 160).

In other cases the stressed vowels of a pair of lines are the same, but the sequence is varied:

> Aquella mora garrida,
> sus amores dan pena a mi vida.
>
> *CMP*, No. 254.

This variation is sometimes caused by the need to conform to the altered rhyme:

> — Digas, morena garrida,
> ¿cuándo serás mi amiga?
> — Cuando esté florida la peña
> d'una flor morena.
>
> Petrus Albertus Vila, *Odarum*, 1571 (text from Alín, No. 621).

Word-repetition

From phonetic parallelism of the above kind it is only a short step to the repetition of words. The lyric commonly repeats a word carrying the main notional emphasis:

> ¡*Tanta* naranja madura,
> *tanto* limón en el suelo,
> *tanta* niña tan bonita,
> *tanta* mocita sin dueño!
>
> Argentina (Magis, p. 378).

> Si yo *cantando, cantando,*
> *cantando* me mantuviera,
> *cantaría* toda la noche
> y hasta que amaneciera.
>
> México (Magis, p. 380).

Conceptual and syntactical parallelism

The binary structure of the lyric, especially that of the four-line forms, lends itself well to parallelism of content and syntax such as that exemplified by

> Adiós, vida de mi vida;
> tu vuelta, ¿quién la irá a ver?
> Ya se van mis tristes ojos;
> mi suerte, ¿cuál irá a ser?
>
> Argentina (Magis, p. 386).

and to the use of simile in a parallel format:

> Mira como corre el agua
> por debajo del laurel;
> así corre la hermosura
> por tu carita, Isabel.
>
> Rodríguez Marín, *Cantos*, No. 1333.

Refrain-repetition

One of the main forms of literal repetition is the refrain. In addition to its importance in those forms (*zéjel, villancico, cosaute*) in which refrain-repetition is integral, the refrain is also used to give cohesion and unity of tone to otherwise unrelated stanzas sung to the same tune:

> ¿Cómo quieres que tenga
> firme esperanza,
> si el cordón que me diste
> ya no me alcanza?
>   Salada morena,
> tú eres el olor de la yerbagüena.
>
> Si quieres que te quiera,
> dame confites,
> que se me han acabado
> los que me diste.
>   Salada . . .

> Algún día los aires
> de la tu casa
> me sirvieron de alivio,
> ahora me matan.
> Salada . . .

Extremadura (García Matos, No. 85).

Line-repetition

Several of the procedures mentioned above (repetition of vowel sequences, reiteration of words, syntactical parallelism) are merged in the literal repetition of lines within the lyric unit. A cornerstone of the lyric's rhetoric is a combination of repetition with variation: the second element of the binary pattern is often a literal repetition of the first, with just enough alteration to make it interesting. This process is seen at its most clear-cut in the two-line *estribillo*, where the alteration in l. 2 is often simply a truncation:

> So ell enzina, enzina,
> so ell enzina.

CMP, No. 20.

> Mano a mano los dos amores,
> mano a mano.

CMP, No. 65.

> Mi ventura, el caballero,
> mi ventura.

CMP, No. 153.

In many cases this truncation results in a line ending in a stressed vowel, and part of the point of the procedure is the contrast between the closing rhythms of the two lines:

> Al alba venid, buen amigo,
> al alba venid.

CMP, No. 7.

No pueden dormir mis ojos,
no pueden dormir.

CMP, No. 114.

In other two-line units, the variation in l. 2 consists of a substitution, again commonly resulting in a contrasting stress-pattern:

Yo me soy la morenica,
yo me soy la morená.

C. Upsala, No. XLIV.

Tómale allá, tu verde olivico;
tómale allá, tu verde olivar.

Correas, *Vocabulario*.

In other cases, there is variation by inversion, sometimes also involving truncation:

De Monçón venía el moço;
moço venía de Monçón.

CMP, No. 34.

Del rosal vengo, mi madre,
vengo del rosale.

Gil Vicente, *Triunfo do verão* (*Obras completas*, Vol. IV, p. 312).

In this last example the assonance is preserved in spite of the variation in l. 2. Other cases of this are rather rare:

Ya viene el alba, niña,
ya viene el día.

Cejador, No. 197.

Por el río me llevad, amigo,
y llevadme por el río.

Gil Vicente, *Cortes de Júpiter* (*Obras completas*, Vol. IV, p. 251).

In the three-line *estribillos* l. 2 may repeat l. 1, or l. 3 may repeat l. 2, but easily the commonest repetition is that of l. 1 by l. 3. One could also perhaps interpret this as a kind of variation by truncation (ll. 1–2, as a unit, being partially repeated by l. 3, as l. 2 partially repeats l. 1 in the two-line *estribillos* above):

> Hilo de oro mana
> la fontana,
> hilo de oro mana.

MS. 4257, fol. 13 (text from Alín, No. 288).

> Si lo dizen, digan,
> alma mía;
> si lo dizen, digan.

CMP, No. 193.

> ¡Mal haya quien los envuelve,
> los mis amores!
> ¡Mal haya quien los envuelve!

Gil Vicente, *Auto dos Quatro Tempos*
(*Obras completas*, Vol. I, p. 102).

Just as in the two-line *estribillo*, the repetition in the three-line forms can be varied by truncation, substitution or inversion:

> Preso está mi corazón,
> preso está,
> mas muerte le librará.

C. general, fol. 147ᵛ.

> Vos me matastes,
> niña en cabello,
> vos m'habéis muerto.

Vásquez, *Recopilación*, I, 15.

Enemiga le soy, madre,
a aquel caballero yo.
¡Mal enemiga le so!

CMP, No. 3.

In the four-line forms, be they *estribillos*, *seguidillas* or octosyllabic *coplas*, the rhythm is basically different. The longer and syllabically more balanced form lends itself to a doubling of the basic pattern, in which repetition of l. 1 in l. 3 is very common, with a more leisurely amplification in ll. 2 and 4 than is possible in the two- and three-line forms:

Vuestros son mis ojos,
Isabel;
vuestros son mis ojos,
y mi corazón también.

CMP, No. 311.

Tirte allá, que no quiero,
mozuelo Rodrigo;
tirte allá, que no quiero
que burles conmigo.

Luis Milán, *El cortesano*, 1561 (text from Alín, p. 349).

Aguamanos pide la niña
para lavarse;
aguamanos pide la niña,
y no se la dane.

Silva de varios romances, 1561 (text from Alín, No. 487).

In the four-line forms, too, we find repetition with variation in ll. 1 and 3:

Que si soy morena,
madre, a la fe,
que si soy morenita,
yo me lo pasaré.

> Juan de Chen, *Laberinto amoroso*, 1618
> (text from Sánchez Romeralo, No. 274).

Dentro en el vergel
moriré.
Dentro en el rosal
matar m'han.

> *CMP*, No. 366.

An important new complication confronts us in those four-line lyrics in which l. 1 is repeated with a variation in l. 3, and l. 2 is repeated with an assonantally linked variation in l. 4, resulting in a doubly parallelistic format in which a single concept is worked out anew in near-paraphrase or with different word-order:

Dame del tu amor, señora,
siquiera una rosa.
Dame del tu amor, galana,
siquiera una rama.

> Mateo Flecha, *Ensaladas*, 1581 (text from
> Alín, No. 682).

Quien piensa que tiene amiga
tiene una higa;
quien piensa que tiene amada
no tiene nada.

> Pedro de Andrade Caminha, *Poesías
> inéditas*, Halle, 1898, No. 398.

¡Ay, madre, la zarzuela,
cómo el aire la revolea!
¡Ay, la zarzuela, madre,
cómo la revolea el aire!

> Extremadura (García Matos, p. 57).

The cosaute

This brief examination of various examples of the lyric's love of reiteration and parallelism has now brought us to a stage where we are only one step away from the most complicated manifestation of these characteristics, the *cosaute*, in which parallelism and repetition, and the structure formed with them, come to constitute the essence of the poem. The thematic content, often no greater than that condensed in a two- or three-line *estribillo* elsewhere, is spun out in an alternating pattern of advance and regression, in which each stanza picks up and slightly develops ideas already expressed, so that the effect is that of a doubly interwoven chain; still a binary pattern, but now one of leisured and hypnotic movement:

> Per ribeyra do rio
> vi remar o navio,
> e sabor ey da ribeyra.
>
> Per ribeyra do alto
> vi remar o barco,
> e sabor ey da ribeyra.
>
> Vi remar o navio;
> hy vay o meu amigo,
> e sabor ey da ribeyra.
>
> Vi remar o barco;
> hy vay o meu amado,
> e sabor ey da ribeyra.
>
> Hy vay o meu amigo;
> quer me levar consigo,
> e sabor ey da ribeyra.
>
> Hy vay o meu amado;
> quer me levar de grado,
> e sabor ey da ribeyra.
>
> Joham Zorro (*CBN*, No. 1095).

Parallelism of this kind is still found in the oral lyric, where it is
sometimes linked with dance movements, and the many medieval
gallego examples, by court poets, are probably imitations of songs to
accompany popular dance-forms. A high proportion of surviving *cosautes*
are in *gallego*; this is partly a consequence of the dominance of *gallego*
as a lyric medium in the medieval courts. In the Golden Age there are
many examples of fully or partly parallelistic poems in Castilian, but
modern field-work, and particularly that of Torner in Asturias, appears
to reinforce the idea that the *cosaute*, while not peculiar to the north-west,
had and has a stronger hold there than elsewhere in the Peninsula (see
Torner, *Lírica*, pp. 405–15). There is a possibility, however, that many
Castilian lyrics in manuscript or printed collections had a parallelistic
structure which is not apparent in the form in which they survive. For
instance, it is possible that a lyric often praised for its brevity,

> En Ávila, mis ojos,
> dentro en Ávila.
>
> En Ávila del Río
> mataron a mi amigo,
> dentro en Ávila.
>
> *CMP*, No. 215.

could have been simply the *estribillo* and first stanza of a poem in
cosaute form which continued, let us say:

> En Ávila del vado
> mataron a mi amado,
> dentro en Ávila . . .[3]

---

[3] For suggestions as to other such possibilities, see Romeu Figueras, 'El cosante . . .'.
For a full study of the rhetoric of the *cosaute*, see Asensio, *Poética y realidad . . .*,
pp. 69–119, 177–215.

Bibliography and List of Abbreviations

WORKS particularly recommended for further reading are marked with an asterisk. This list includes only works either not mentioned elsewhere in the book or cited in the notes in an abbreviated form. Works to which reference is made only once or twice in the notes are cited there *in extenso*, and are not included here.

*Alín.   ALÍN, J. M., *El cancionero español de tipo tradicional*, Madrid, 1968.
Alonso Cortés.   ALONSO CORTÉS, N., 'Cantares populares de Castilla', *Revue Hispanique*, XXXII (1914), pp. 87–427.
Álvarez.   ÁLVAREZ, G., *El habla de Babia y Laciana*, Madrid, 1949.
Álvarez Gato.   ÁLVAREZ GATO, JUAN, *Obras completas*, ed. Jenaro Artiles, Madrid, 1928.
*Antología.   ALONSO, DÁMASO and BLECUA, J. M., *Antología de la poesía española. Poesía de tipo tradicional*, Madrid, 1956.
*ASENSIO, E., *Poética y realidad en el cancionero peninsular de la Edad Media*, 2nd ed., Madrid, 1970.
CBN.   *Cancioneiro da Biblioteca Nacional*, ed. Machado, E. P. and Machado, J. P., 8 vols., Lisbon, 1949–64.
C. Colombina.   *Cancionero musical de la Biblioteca Colombina de Sevilla* (described in Romeu Figueras, J., 'La poesía popular en los cancioneros . . . ' (see p. 39)).
Cejador.   CEJADOR Y FRAUCA, J., *La verdadera poesía castellana*, Vols. I–V, Madrid, 1921–4.
C. galanes.   *Cancionero de galanes*, 1520, ed. Frenk Alatorre, M., Valencia, 1952.
C. general.   *Cancionero general de Hernando del Castillo*, Valencia, 1511 (facsimile edition by A. Rodríguez-Moñino, Madrid, 1958).
C. Horozco.   *Cancionero de Sebastián de Horozco*, ed. Bibliófilos Andaluces, Seville, 1874.
CMP. *Cancionero musical de Palacio*, ed. Anglés, H., 2 vols., Barcelona, 1947–51.
Correas, *Arte*.   CORREAS, G., *Arte grande de la lengua española castellana*, ed. Alarcos García, E., Madrid, 1954.
Correas, *Vocabulario*.   CORREAS, G., *Vocabulario de refranes y frases proverbiales*, ed. Real Academia Española, Madrid, 1906. No page references are given for this work, as its alphabetical arrangement makes them superfluous.
C. sevillano.   A collection described by FRENK ALATORRE, M. in 'El *Cancionero sevillano* de la Hispanic Society (*ca.* 1568)', *Nueva Revista de Filología Hispánica*, XVI (1962), pp. 355–94.

C. Upsala.   *Cancionero de Upsala*, Venice, 1556, ed. Mitjana, R., Mexico, 1944.

Foulché-Delbosc, 'Séguedilles'.   FOULCHÉ-DELBOSC, R., 'Séguedilles anciennes', *Revue Hispanique*, VIII (1901), pp. 309–31.

*FRENK ALATORRE, M., 'Dignificación de la lírica popular en el Siglo de Oro', *Anuario de Letras*, Mexico, 1962, pp. 27–54.

FRENK ALATORRE, M., 'Glosas de tipo popular en la antigua lírica', *Nueva Revista de Filología Hispánica*, XII (1958), pp. 301–34.

FRENK ALATORRE, M., 'Sobre los textos poéticos en Juan Vásquez, Mudarra y Narváez', *Nueva Revista de Filología Hispánica*, VI (1952), pp. 33–56.

*Frenk Alatorre, 'Supervivencias'.   FRENK ALATORRE, M., 'Supervivencias de la antigua lírica popular', *Homenaje a Dámaso Alonso*, Madrid, 1960, Vol. I, pp. 51–78.

*García Gómez.   GARCÍA GÓMEZ, E. *Las jarchas romances de la serie árabe en su marco*, Madrid, 1965.

García Lorca, *Obras*.   GARCÍA LORCA, FEDERICO, *Obras completas*, 9th ed., Madrid (Aguilar), 1965.

García Matos.   GARCÍA MATOS, M., *Lírica popular de la Alta Extremadura*, Madrid, 1944.

LE GENTIL, P., *Le virelai et le villancico*, Paris, 1954.

LE GENTIL, P., 'Strophe zadjalesque, les khardjas et le problème des origines du lyrisme roman', *Romania*, LXXXIV (1963), pp. 1–27, 209–50.

LOPE DE VEGA, *Obras*, 15 vols., Madrid, 1890–1913; 2nd series, 13 vols., Madrid, 1916–30.

Magis.   MAGIS, CARLOS H., *La lírica popular contemporánea: España, México, Argentina*, México, 1969.

*MENÉNDEZ PIDAL, R., 'La primitiva lírica europea. Estado actual del problema', *Revista de Filología Española*, XLIII, 1960, pp. 279–354.

Mingote.   MINGOTE, A., *Cancionero musical de la provincia de Zaragoza*, Zaragoza, 1950.

Molina.   MOLINA, R., *Cante flamenco*, Madrid, 1965; 2nd ed., Madrid, 1969.

MS. . . .   Sixteenth- and seventeenth-century manuscript collections in the Biblioteca Nacional, Madrid, Nos. 2478, 3168, 3890, 3915, 3924, 4072, 4257, 5593, 14,088, 17,698.

*NUNES, J. J., *Cantigas d'amigo dos trovadores gallego-portugueses*, 3 vols., Coimbra, 1926–8.

POHREN, D. E., *El arte del flamenco*, Morón de la Frontera, 1970.

*Reckert.   RECKERT, S., *Lyra Minima. Structure and Symbol in Iberian Traditional Verse*, London, 1970.

Rodríguez Marín, *Cantos*.   RODRÍGUEZ MARÍN, F., *Cantos populares españoles*, 2nd ed., 5 vols., Madrid, 1951.

Rodríguez Marín, *Refranes*.   RODRÍGUEZ MARÍN, F., *Más de 21.000 refranes castellanos*, Madrid, 1926.

'Romancerillos'.   FOULCHÉ-DELBOSC, R., 'Romancerillos de Pise', *Revue Hispanique*, LXV (1925), pp. 160–263.

ROMEU FIGUERAS, J., 'El cantar paralelístico en Cataluña. Sus relaciones con el de Galicia y Portugal y el de Castilla', *Anuario Musical* (1954), pp. 3–55.

*ROMEU FIGUERAS, J., 'El cosante en la lírica de los cancioneros musicales españoles de los siglos XV y XVI', *Anuario Musical* (1950), pp. 15–61.

ROMEU FIGUERAS, J., 'La poesía popular en los cancioneros musicales españoles de los siglos XV y XVI', *Anuario Musical* (1949), pp. 57–91.

Sánchez de Badajoz, *Recopilación*. SÁNCHEZ DE BADAJOZ, Diego, *Recopilación en metro*, 1554, ed. Real Academia Española, Madrid, 1929.

*SÁNCHEZ ROMERALO, A., *El villancico*, Madrid, 1969.

*Schindler. SCHINDLER, K., *Folk Music and Poetry of Spain and Portugal*, New York, 1941.

Sevilla. SEVILLA, A., *Cancionero popular murciano*, Murcia, 1921.

STERN, J. M., *Les chansons mozarabes*, Palermo, 1953.

Tonos castellanos. MSS. 13,230 and 13,231, Biblioteca del Palacio de Medinaceli, Madrid.

*Torner, *Cancionero*. TORNER, E. MARTÍNEZ, *Cancionero musical de la lírica popular asturiana*, Madrid, 1920; reprinted Oviedo, 1971.

*Torner, 'Indice'. TORNER, E. MARTÍNEZ, 'Indice de analogías entre la lírica española antigua y la moderna', *Symposium*, I (1947), No. 1, pp. 12–33; No. 2, pp. 4–35; No. 3, pp. 84–107; II (1948), pp. 84–105, 221–41; III (1949), pp. 282–320; IV (1950), pp. 141–80.

*Torner, *Lírica*. TORNER, E. MARTÍNEZ, *Lírica hispánica. Relaciones entre lo popular y lo culto*, Madrid, 1966.

Torres Villarroel. TORRES VILLARROEL, DIEGO DE, *Obras*, 15 vols., Madrid, 1794–9.

Vásquez, *Recopilación*. VÁSQUEZ, JUAN, *Recopilación de sonetos y villancicos a quatro y a cinco*, Seville, 1560, ed. Anglés, H., Barcelona, 1946.

Vásquez, *Villancicos*. VÁSQUEZ, JUAN, *Villancicos y canciones a tres y a quatro*, Osuna, 1551.

VICENTE, GIL, *Obras completas*, ed. Marques Braga, 6 vols., Lisbon, 1942–4.

Zafra, *Villancicos*. ZAFRA, ESTEBAN DE, *Villancicos para cantar en la Natividad de Nuestro Señor Jesucristo*, Toledo, 1545.

PART I

An anthology of traditional verse, covering the period from the eleventh century to the present day.

A quien no agradaren
las seguidillas,
denle con un palo
por las costillas.

Foulché-Delbosc, 'Séguedilles', No. 285.

¡Ay amor, amor, ay amante!

From its earliest manifestations to the present day, the traditional lyric's principal theme is love. In a large majority of cases, the viewpoint on love is a feminine one, and the poem, often addressed to the beloved, expresses some aspect of love's joy or misery. One of the lyric's commonest understatements is the use of the word *amigo* to denote the beloved. This usage is almost inevitable in medieval *gallego* lyrics (where the parallelistic form often necessitates the *amigo/amado* variation), and is not uncommon in Castilian poems. The corresponding form in the Mozarabic lyric is the Arabic word *ḥabīb*.

The sexual side of love, only rarely referred to with directness, nevertheless gives depth and solidity to the lyric. For a society basically rural, steeped in the awareness that existence depends on husbanding and preserving the productiveness of animal and soil, human sexual activity is accepted as part of an overall fertility, to ignore which is unthinkable. The lyric's chief beauty is the delicacy with which it treats this basic and inescapable theme, occasionally lightening it with humour, but more often making deft use of a natural symbolism which illuminates human fertility as an aspect of a wider continuity. Certain motifs of this symbolism are accorded separate sections elsewhere in Part I.

1

Tant' amắre, tant' amắre,
ḥabīb, tant' amắre,
enfermíron welyos nídios
e dólen tan mắlē.

García Gómez, Apéndice 1°, 18.

A Mozarabic *kharja*, thought to be pre-1042, and consequently the oldest extant romance lyric.

In ll. 1–2 *amắre* is infinitive, though *tan te mirai*, 'I looked at you so much', is a possible reading; l. 3, *enfermíron welyos*, 'my eyes fell ill'; *nídios*, 'clear, bright'? (a doubtful form, perhaps < *nitidos*, although other interpretations of the script have been suggested, including *belidos*, 'fine, beautiful').

43

2

Amad' e meu amigo,
¡valha Deus!,
vede la frol do pinho
e guisade d' andar.

5 Amigu e meu amado,
¡valha Deus!,
vede la frol do ramo
e guisade d' andar.

Vede la frol do pinho,
10 ¡valha Deus!,
selad' o baiosinho
e guisade d' andar.

Vede la frol do ramo,
¡valha Deus!,
15 selad' o bel cavalo
e guisade d' andar.

Selad' o baiosinho,
¡valha Deus!,
treide-vos, ay amigo,
20 e guisade d' andar.

Selad' o bel cavalo,
¡valha Deus!,
treide-vos, ay amado,
e guisade d' andar.

King Denis of Portugal, 1261–1325 (*CBN*,
No. 535).

l. 2, etc., *¡valha Deus!*, 'God save you!'; l. 3, *vede la frol do pinho*, 'see the flower of the pine'; l. 4, *guisade d'*, 'make ready to'; l. 11, *selad' o baiosinho*, 'saddle the little bay horse'; l. 19, *treide-vos*, 'come'.

3

Si lo dizen, digan,
alma mía,
si lo dizen, digan.

Dizen que vos quiero
5 y por vos me muero:
dicho es verdadero,
alma mía,
si lo dizen, digan.

CMP, No. 193.

4

Vos me matastes,
niña en cabello,
vos m'habéis muerto.

Ribera d'un río
5 vi moza virgo;
niña en cabello,
vos m'habéis muerto.
Vos me matastes,
niña en cabello.

Vásquez, *Recopilación*, I, 15.

The 'niña en cabello' is the girl with her hair uncut and flowing down, the maiden or virgin. The convention persisted until recently by which a girl did not put up her hair until she married. Cf. this wedding song from Asturias: Casadina, bien llegada, / serás bien arrecibida; / bien venida la casada, / la casada bien venida. / Ayer estabas soltera / con el cabello tendido, / y ahora estás prisionera / a la sombra del marido. (Torner, *Lírica*, No. 44.)

5

Véante mis ojos,
y muérame yo luego,
dulce amor mío
y lo que yo más quiero.

Jorge de Montemayor, *Cancionero*, 1553
(text from Alín, No. 385).

6

Tres morillas m'enamoran
en Jaén,
Axa y Fátima y Marién.

Tres morillas tan garridas
5   iban a coger olivas,
y hallábanlas cogidas
en Jaén,
Axa y Fátima y Marién.

Y hallábanlas cogidas,
10   y tornaban desmaídas
y las colores perdidas
en Jaén,
Axa y Fátima y Marién.

Tres moricas tan loçanas,
15   tres moricas tan loçanas
iban a coger mançanas
a Jaén,
Axa y Fátima y Marién.

CMP, No. 24.

l. 10, *desmaídas*, 'pale, faint'.

7

Ojos morenos,
¿cuándo nos veremos?

Ojos morenos,
de bonica color,
5   soys tan graciosos
que matáis d'amor.
¿Cuándo nos veremos,
ojos morenos?

Vásquez, Recopilación, I, 21.

8

Hícele la cama
a mi enamorado,
hícele la cama
sobre mi costado.

C. sevillano, fol. 48.

9

A sombra de mis cabellos
se adurmió:
¿si le recordaré yo?

CMP, No. 360.

Cf. this *estribillo* from the Canaries: A la sombra del cabello / de mi dama, dormí un sueño. (Torner, *Lírica*, No. 11.)

10

Besóme el colmenero,
y a la miel me supo el beso.

Correas, Vocabulario.

11

Ojos morenicos,
irm'é yo a querellar,
que me queredes matar.

Quexarm'é de mí
5 que ansí me vencí,
que desque os vi
me aquexó el pesar.
Que me queredes matar.

CMP, No. 263.

12

¡Quedito! No me toquéis,
entrañas mías,
que tenéis las manos frías.

Yo os doy mi fe que venís
5 esta noche tan helado,
que si vos no lo sentís,
de sentido estáis privado.
No toquéis en lo vedado,
entrañas mías,
10 que tenéis las manos frías.

MS. 4072, fol. 10.

13

Soy toquera
y vendo tocas,
y tengo mi cofre
donde las otras.

Correas, *Arte*, p. 455.

14

Que no me desnudéys,
amores de mi vida;
que no me desnudéys,
que yo me yré en camisa.

5   Entrastes, mi señora,
    en el huerto ageno,
    cogistes tres pericas
    del peral del medio;
    dexaredes la prenda
10 d'amor verdadero.
    Que no me desnudéys,
    que yo me yré en camisa.

Vásquez, *Recopilación*, II, 39.

¡Ay, ay, ay, ay! ¡qué fuerte mal!

There are several conventional variations on the *chagrin d'amour*
theme. The broken appointment, the failure of the lover to appear at
the promised *plazo*, occurs repeatedly. In other poems he comes late,
giving rise to the girl's speculations about his possible unfaithfulness; in
others his deceit is proven. Sleeplessness is a common element; it may
be linked with unfaithfulness or neglect, or may be caused merely by the
depth of the girl's love, or by a vaguely perceived desire for fulfilment.
Separation is another frequent cause of misery; the leave-taking may be
for only a short time, or the lover may be going away with little hope of
return, perhaps as a prisoner in the galleys, or to serve in the army
or the king's ships. The themes of sleeplessness and separation may
each overlap the *alba* theme (see Nos. 15, 26, 37, 40).

15

Aṣ-ṣabāḥ bōnō, gār-mē de 'ón bénĕš.
Yā lo šé k'ōtrī amaš,
e mībī non qēreš.

García Gómez, Apéndice 1°, 17.

A Mozarabic *kharja* of the thirteenth century.
l. 1, *Aṣ-ṣabāḥ* (Arabic), 'dawn'; *gār-mē de 'ón bénĕš*, 'tell me from where you come';
l. 2, *ōtrī*, 'another'; l. 3, *mībī non qēreš*, 'you do not love me'.

16

Non chegou, madre, o meu amigo,
e oi est o prazo saydo.
¡Ay, madre, moyro d'amor!

Non chegou, madre, o meu amado,
5 e oi est o prazo passado.
¡Ay, madre, moyro d'amor!

E oi est o prazo saydo.
¿Por que mentiu o desmentido?
¡Ay, madre, moyro d'amor!

10 E oi est o prazo passado.
¿Por que mentiu o perjurado?
¡Ay, madre, moyro d'amor!

Por que mentiu o desmentido,
pesa-mi, poys per si é falido.
15 ¡Ay, madre, moyro d'amor!

Por que mentiu o perjurado,
pesa-mi, poys mentiu per seu grado.
¡Ay, madre, moyro d'amor!

King Denis of Portugal (*CBN*, No. 531).

l. 1, *Non chegou*, 'has not arrived'; *o meu*, 'my'; l. 2, *oi est o prazo saydo*, 'today the time-limit expires', 'this is the day appointed'; l. 3, *moyro*, 'I am dying'; l. 14, *poys per si é falido*, 'because he has failed me, and the blame is his' (or perhaps 'because he is diminished in my eyes through his own fault').

17

Dizia la fremosinha:
¡Ay, Deus val!
¡com estou d'amor ferida!
¡Ay, Deus val!

5 Dizia la ben talhada:
¡Ay, Deus val!
¡com estou d'amor coytada!
¡Ay, Deus val!

E com estou d'amor ferida,
10 ¡Ay, Deus val!
non ven o que ben queria,
¡Ay, Deus val!

E com estou d'amor coytada,
¡Ay, Deus val!
15 non ven o que muyto amava,
¡Ay, Deus val!

Alfonso Sanches (*CBN*, No. 726).

l. 1, *fremosinha*, 'pretty young girl'; l. 2, *¡Ay, Deus val!*, 'God help me!'; l. 5, *ben talhada*, 'shapely girl'; l. 7, *coytada*, 'pained, stricken'; l. 11, *non ven o que ben queria*, 'the one whom I love(d) deeply does not come'.

18

Puse mis amores
en Fernandico.
¡Ay, que era casado!
¡Mal me ha mentido!

5 Digas, marinero
del cuerpo garrido,
¿en cuál de aquellas naves
pasa Fernandico?
¡Ay, que era casado!
10 ¡Mal me ha mentido!
Puse mis amores
en Fernandico.

Vásquez, *Villancicos* (text from *Antología*, No. 93).

l. 6, *garrido*, 'fine, bonny'.

19

Que todos se pasan en flores,
mis amores.

Las flores que han nascido
del tiempo que os he servido,
5 derribólas vuestro olvido
y disfavores.
Que todos se pasan en flores,
mis amores.

C. Upsala, No. XII.

20

Por el val que habéis de arar,
el desposado,
por el val que habéis de arar
ya estaba arado.

Gabriel Lasso de la Vega, *Manojuelo de
romances*, ed. E. Mele and A.
González Palencia, Madrid, 1942,
No. 92.

21

Aunque siempre estoy cantando,
no crean que no tengo pena.
Tengo yo mi corazón
como las moritas negras.

San Martín del Pimpollar, Ávila
(Schindler, p. 118).

22

El amor del soldado
no es más de una hora,
que en tocando la caja,
¡y adiós, señora!

Correas, *Vocabulario*.

Cf. this modern version from Argentina: Amor de forastero / no dura una hora;
/ ensilla su caballo / y '¡Adiós, señora!', and other similar poems in Torner, *Lírica*,
No. 162.

23

Si la noche haze escura
y tan corto es el camino,
¿cómo no venís, amigo?

C. galanes, p. 57.

24

Esta noche y la pasada,
¿cómo no has venido, mi amor,
estando la luna clara
y el caminito andador?

Santander (Schindler, No. 532).

25

No pueden dormir mis ojos,
no pueden dormir.

Y soñaba yo, mi madre,
dos horas antes del día,
5   que me floreçía la rosa,
ell vino so ell agua frida.
No pueden dormir.

CMP, No. 114.

26

Cantan los gallos;
yo no me duermo
ni tengo sueño.

Gil Vicente, *Farsa de Quem tem farelos?*,
Obras completas, Vol. V, p. 78.

Cf. a modern song from Asturias (Torner, 'Indice', No. 44): Canta el gallu, canta
el gallu, / canta el gallu y amanéz; / la neña que tién amores / tarde o nunca se
adorméz.

27
El agua del río corre,
la del arroyo remansa;
quien tiene amores no duerme,
quien no los tiene descansa.

5 Amante mío del alma,
el sueño no me alimenta:
estoy durmiendo en la cama
y la pena me dispierta.

Asturias (Torner, *Lírica*, No. 198).

The same section in Torner contains many other lyrics of sleeplessness.

The mother

In a high proportion of poems, including many in sections other than
this, the words of the girl are addressed to her mother, who may be a
sympathetic confidante, but is commonly a hostile figure, a hindrance
to the love-affair. In the shorter Castilian lyrics, the mother rarely
speaks herself, but dialogues between mother and daughter often occur
in the Galician *cosaute*, whose parallelistic form is peculiarly suitable
for this mode of presentation.

28
¿Ké faré, mamma?
Me-u l-ḥabīb ešt 'ad yana.

García Gómez, Apéndice 1°, No. 14.

l. 1, *¿Ké faré?*, 'What shall I do?'; l. 2, *Me-u l-ḥabīb ešt 'ad yana*, 'My lover is at the
door'.
The proportion of the extant *kharjas* in which the mother is addressed is high (see
García Gómez, Nos. X, XIV, XV, XVII, XIX, XXI, XXX, XXXI, XXXIII, XXXIV;
Apéndice 1°, Nos. 11, 22).

29
— Digades, filha, mha filha velida,
¿porque tardastes na fontana fría?
— Os amores ey.

— Digades, filha, mha filha louçana,
5 ¿porque tardastes na fria fontana?
— Os amores ey.

Tardei, mha madre, na fontana fria,
cervos do monte a augua volvian.
Os amores ey.

10 Tardei, mha madre, na fria fontana,
cervos do monte volvian a augua.
Os amores ey.

— Mentir, mha filha, mentir por amigo.
Nunca vi cervo que volvess' o rio.
15 — Os amores ey.

Mentir, mha filha, mentir por amado.
Nunca vi cervo que volvess' o alto.
— Os amores ey.

Pero Meõgo (*CBN*, No. 1140).

l. 1, *filha*, 'daughter'; *mha*, 'my'; *velida*, 'fine, comely'; l. 2, *na*, 'in the'; l. 8, *cervos*, 'stags'; *do*, 'of the'; *a augua volvian*, 'were stirring up the water'; l. 17, *o alto*, 'the deep water'.

30
Aquel caballero, madre,
que de amores me fabló,
más que a mí le quiero yo.

CMP, No. 329.

Cf. this oral version, collected four centuries later in Sotillo del Rincón, Soria: Aquel caballero, madre, / que de mí se enamoró, / habiéndole dado el sí, / ¿cómo le daré yo el no? (Schindler, No. 838).

31
No tengo cabellos, madre,
mas tengo bonico donaire.

No tengo cabellos, madre,
que me lleguen a la cinta;
5 mas tengo bonico donaire
con que mato a quien me mira.

Mato a quien me mira, madre,
con mi bonico donaire.
No tengo cabellos, madre,
10 mas tengo bonico donaire.

Vásquez, *Recopilación*, II, 38.

See above, No. 4, note.

32

Cuando le veo
el amor, madre,
toda se arrevuelve
la mi sangre.

MS. 17,698, No. 34.

33

Llaman a Teresica
y no viene.
¡Qué mala noche tiene!

Llámale su madre,
5 y ella calla;
juramento haze
de matalla.
¡Qué mala noche tiene!

MS. 2478 (text from Alín, No. 342).

l. 7, *matalla* is an old form of *matarla*.

34

No me firáys, madre,
yo os lo diré;
mal d'amores hé.

Madre, un caballero
5   de casa del rey,
siendo yo muy niña
pidióme la fe;
dísela yo, madre,
no lo negaré.
10   Mal d'amores hé.
No me firáys, madre,
yo os lo diré:
mal d'amores hé.

Vásquez, *Recopilación*, II, 32.

l. 1, *no me firáys*, 'don't hit me'.

35

Madre, la mi madre,
guardas me ponéis;
que si yo no me guardo,
mal me guardaréis.

Correas, *Arte*, p. 453.

This poem is used by Cervantes in *El celoso extremeño*, the theme of which it largely summarizes.

36

Con la luna, madre, con la luna iré;
con el sol no quiero, que me quemaré;
que me quemaré, que me quemaré;
con la luna, madre, con la luna iré.

Diustes, Soria (Schindler, No. 646).

The dawn

The theme of dawn (sunrise, cock-crow, awakening) is a factor in both the traditional lyric and the medieval courtly lyric, and the possibility of interaction between the two cannot be discounted. In the court lyric, especially in French, the *aubade* is a minor facet of the courtly convention, often involving the separation of the illicit lovers in face of the threat of discovery. Separation is only one side of the *alba* theme in the traditional lyric; quite commonly dawn is the time of meeting or arrival, or of the awakening of one lover by the other.

37

Non dormiréyo, mammā,
a rāyyo d̠ē manyānā,
ben Abū-l-Qāsim,
la fāže d̠ē maṭrānā.

García Gómez, No. XVII.

A Mozarabic *kharja*, probably of the eleventh century (García Gómez, No. XIX includes a different version of the same lyric).
l. 1, *Non dormiréyo*, 'I shall not sleep'; l. 3, *ben*, 'comes' (this form, however, involves a tinkering with the Arabic text in order to provide a verb; *buen* is more justified by the manuscript); l. 4, *la fāže d̠ē maṭrānā*, 'the face of the dawn'.

38

Levad' amigo, que dormides as manhanas frias;
toda-las aves do mundo d'amor dizian.
Leda m' and' eu.

Levad' amigo, que dormides as frias manhanas;
5 toda-las aves do mundo d'amor cantavan.
Leda m' and' eu.

Toda-las aves do mundo d'amor dizian;
do meu amor e do voss' en ment' avian.
Leda m' and' eu.

10 Toda-las aves do mundo d'amor cantavan;
do meu amor e do voss' y enmentavan.
Leda m' and' eu.

Do meu amor e do voss' en ment' avian;
vos lhi tolhestes os ramos en que siian.
15 Leda m' and' eu.

Do meu amor e do voss' y enmentavan;
vos lhi tolhestes os ramos en que pousavan.
Leda m' and' eu.

Vos lhi tolhestes os ramos en que siian,
20 e lhis secastes as fontes en que bevian.
Leda m' and' eu.

Vos lhi tolhestes os ramos en que pousavan,
e lhis secastes as fontes hu se banhavan.
Leda m' and' eu.

Nuno Fernandez Torneol (*CBN*, No. 604).

l. 1, *Levad'*, 'Get up'; l. 2, *toda-las*, 'all the'; l. 3, *Leda m' and' eu*, 'I am [literally 'go'] joyful'; l. 8, *do meu amor y do voss' en ment' avian*, 'they were thinking of my love and yours'; l. 14, *vos lhi tolhestes*, 'you took away (or 'cut off') from them'; l. 23, *hu*, 'where'.

This poem is the subject of a study by G. Tavani, *Poesia del duecento nella Penisola Iberica*, Rome, 1969, pp. 265–74. The joyful refrain presents a problem, appearing to jar with the melancholy content of the second half of the poem, unless one could perhaps interpret the imagery of the last four stanzas as indicating the devastating profundity of love, rather than a love withdrawn.

39

Al alba venid, buen amigo,
al alba venid.

Amigo el que yo más quería,
venid al alba del día.

5 Amigo el que yo más amaba,
venid a la luz del alba.

Venid a la luz del día,
non trayáis compañía.

Venid a la luz del alba,
10 non traigáis gran compaña.

CMP, No. 7.

40

Cantan os galos o día;
meu amor, érguete e vaite.
— ¿Cómo m' hei d' ir, queridiña,
cómo m' hei d' ir e deixarte?

Galicia (Torner, *Lírica*, No. 52).

l. 1, *os galos*, 'the cocks'; l. 2, *érguete e vaite*, 'get up and go'; l. 3, *¿Cómo m' hei d' ir ?*, 'How am I to go?'

41

Ya cantaron los gallos,
ya viene el día;
cada cual a su casa,
y yo a la mía.

Argentina (Torner, *Lírica*, No. 52).

Ribericas del rio

Some of the revelations concerning dream-association for which
Sigmund Freud felt compelled to apologize in advance to the female
members of his audience would have aroused neither blush nor surprise
in anyone acquainted with the motifs of the traditional lyric. The frequent
incidence of the spring or river as an erotic element in the lyric, for
instance, provides convincing support for the Freudian association of
running water with generation and birth. The river-bank is commonly
a lovers' meeting-place, and the erotic connotations are often
strengthened by such elements as the stag disturbing the water (see Nos.
29, 86), the washing of the girl's hair in the stream, and especially by
the bathing of the two lovers together in the *baños de amor*; see also
the series of versions of *Al pasar el arroyo*, pp. 8–13.

42

Fuy eu, madre, lavar meus capelos
a la fonte, e paguey-m' eu d' elos.
¡E de mi,
louçana, é!

5 Fuy eu, madre, lavar mhas garcetas
a la fonte, e paguey-m' eu d' elas.
¡E de mi,
louçana, é!

A la fonte paguey-m' eu d' eles;
10 alá achey, madre, o senhor d' eles.
¡E de mi,
louçana, é!

Ante que m' eu d' ali partisse,
fui pagada do que m' el disse.
15 ¡E de mi,
louçana, é!

Joham Soarez Coelho (*CBN*, No. 652).

l. 1, *eu*, 'I'; *capelos*, 'hair'; l. 2, *fonte*, 'spring'; *paguey-m' eu d' elos*, 'I was pleased with them' (i.e. 'the hair'); l. 4, *louçana*, 'youthful and lively'; l. 5, *garcetas*, 'hair (worn hanging down the cheeks)'; l. 10, *alá achey*, 'there I found'; *o*, 'the'; l. 13, *ali*, 'there'; l. 14, *do que m' el disse*, 'with what he said to me'.

43

A mi puerta nace una fonte;
¿por dó saliré que no me moje?

A mi puerta la garrida
nasce una fonte frida,
5 donde lavo la mi camisa
y la de aquel que yo más quería.
¿Por dó saliré que no me moje?

C. galanes, p. 74.

l. 3, *garrida*, 'fine, bonny'; l. 4, *fonte frida*, 'cold spring'.

44

Mano a mano los dos amores,
mano a mano.

El galán y la galana
ambos vuelven ell agua clara,
5 mano a mano.

CMP, No. 65.

45

A los baños dell amor
sola m'iré,
y en ellos me bañaré.

Porque sane deste mal
5   que me causa desventura,
qu'es un dolor tan mortal
que destruye mi figura.
A los baños de tristura
sola m'iré,
10   y en ellos me bañaré.

CMP, No. 149.

Correas, *Vocabulario*, quotes the proverb: La que del baño viene, bien sabe lo que quiere ('Juntarse con el varón').

46

Si te vas a bañar, Juanica,
dime a cuáles baños vas.

Juanica, cuerpo garrido.

Diego Pisador, *Libro de música de vihuela*,
Salamanca, 1552, fol. XIIII^v (text from
Alín, No. 379).

It is probable that l. 3 is just the beginning of a longer gloss.

47

En la fuente del rosel
lavan la niña y el doncel.

En la fuente de agua clara
con sus manos lavan la cara,
5   él a ella y ella a él;
lavan la niña y el doncel.
En la fuente del rosel
lavan la niña y el doncel.

Vásquez, *Recopilación*, II, 42.

48

Isabel, Isabel,
perdiste la tu faxa;
héla por do va
nadando por el agua;
5 ¡Isabel la tan garrida!

Alonso Mudarra, *Tres libros de música en cifra para vihuela*, 1546, ed. E. Pujol, Barcelona, 1949, No. 73.

49

Orillicas del río
mis amores he,
y debajo de los álamos
me atend[r]é.

Sebastián de Covarrubias, *Tesoro de la lengua castellana o española*, 1611, ed. M. de Riquer, Barcelona, 1943, p. 163.

l, 4, *me atend*[r]*é*, 'I shall wait'. In Covarrubias, where this text is quoted as an example of *atender* meaning 'to wait', the form is *me atendé*. The form without the *r* could perhaps be explained as (a) a 1st-person preterite, with an analogical ending supported by the rhyme, or (b) a 3rd-person present of *atender*, 'to await', with stress dislocated by the rhyme, and consequent reversion of the stem diphthong to a single vowel. Both these solutions are highly questionable. A future tense makes good sense in the context.

50

¿Quién quiere entrar conmigo en el río?
¿Quién quiere entrar conmigo a nadar?
— Yo que no sé nadar, morenita,
yo que no sé nadar, moriré.

Castilfrío de la Sierra, Soria (Schindler, No. 607).

51

A los rayos del sol se peina mi amor;
se viste y se calza del mismo color.

¡Ay de mí! que me lleva la toca el rido;
bájateme por ella, galán querido.
5   A los rayos del sol se peina mi amor;
se viste y se calza del mismo color.

¡Ay de mí! que me lleva la toca el agua;
bájateme por ella, galán del alma.
A los rayos del sol se peina mi amor;
10   se viste y se calza del mismo color.

Infiesto, Asturias (Torner, 'Indice', No. 186).

A dancing-song in *cosaute* form, recorded in this century.
l. 3, *rido*, 'river'.

El aire de amores

The wind has always been an object of mystery to peasant societies, and its inexplicable, ungovernable nature has given rise to numerous superstitions and folk-beliefs. In the traditional lyric the wind, while playing a subsidiary role as an image of freedom or a link with the exile's home-land (see Nos. 237, 240), is more important as a sexual symbol. It acts like a playful, unruly lover, lifting the young girl's skirts; the man prays for a wind to blow him into those skirts; to be burned by the wind is a frequent metaphor for love-making, particularly for the loss of virginity. García Lorca uses this image of the *viento hombrón* in *Preciosa y el aire*, a poem in the *Romancero gitano*. Some of the tree images for love-making also involve the wind (see Nos. 69, 70). In contrast to this disturbing, virile character, the wind occasionally has a more soothing function, lulling the girl or her lover to sleep by rustling the leaves; it plays a similar role in lullabies.

52
Las mis penas, madre,
d'amores son.

Salid, mi señora,
de so'l naranjale,
5   que sois tan hermosa,
quemarvos ha ell aire;
d'amores son.

CMP, No. 59.

Alín (No. 75) suggests 'qu'amarvos' for l. 6; there is no justification for this, and it would destroy an image for which there is support in No. 59 below.
l. 4, *de so'l*, 'from under the'.

53

Estos mis cabellos, madre,
dos a dos me los lleva el aire.

No sé qué pendencia es ésta
del aire con mis cabellos,
5   o si enamorado d'ellos
les hace regalo y fiesta;
de tal suerte los molesta
que cogidos al desgaire
dos a dos me los lleva el aire.

10   Y si acaso los descojo,
luego el aire los maltrata;
también me los desbarata
cuando los entrezo y cojo.
Ora sienta d'esto enojo,
15   ora lo lleve en donaire,
dos a dos me los lleva el aire.

MS. 3915, fol. 69^v.

54

Agora viniese un viento
que me echase acullá dentro.

Agora viniese un viento
tan bueno como querría
5 que me echase acullá dentro
en faldas de mi amiga.
Y me hiciese tan contento
que me echase acullá dentro.

Luis Milán, *Libro de música de vihuela de mano intitulado El Maestro*, 1535 (text from *Antología*, No. 375).

55

¡O, qué venteciño
anda en aquel valle!
Déxame, carillejo,
yr a buscalle.

C. sevillano, fol. 40.

l. 1, *venteciño*, 'little wind'; l. 4, *buscalle*, archaic form of *buscarle*.

56

Levantóse un viento
que de la mar salía,
y alzóme la falda
de mi camisa.

Correas, *Vocabulario*.

57

Un mal ventecillo
loquillo con mis faldas;
¡tira allá, mal viento!
¿qué me las alzas?

Cancionero classense, 1589 (text from **Alín**, No. 714).

l. 2, *loquillo*, 'playful, mischievous'.

58

Airecillo en los mis cabellos,
y aire en ellos.

Correas, *Vocabulario*.

59

Por el río del amor, madre,
que yo blanca me era, blanca,
y quemóme el aire.

Bibliotèque Nationale, Paris, MS. 371
(1595) (text from Alín, No. 742).

60

Ventezillo murmurador,
que lo andas y gozas todo,
hazme el son
con las hojas del olmo
5   mientras duerme mi lindo amor.

'Romancerillos', No. 99.

61

Con el viento murmuran,
madre, las hojas,
y al sonido me duermo
bajo su sombra.

Romancero general, 1604, ed. A.
González Palencia, Madrid, 1947, No.
1028.

62

En la cumbre, madre,
tal aire me dió,
que el amor que tenía
aire se volvió.

Ibid., No. 894.

So ell enzina, enzina

Trees and flowers, in addition to providing an idyllic pastoral setting for the lovers' rendezvous or a shelter for their love-making, are often laden with symbolism. The irresistible urge of the sap, the fascinating but vaguely disturbing process of bud and leaf and flower, are linked, overtly or otherwise, with the burgeoning of the beauty of the girl, her compelling desire for fulfilment, and the birth of love.

Different trees and flowers have different associations. The rose is inextricably bound up with European conventions of the symbolism of love; repeatedly the girl is picking roses or is under a rose-tree when her lover appears. The orange is more peculiarly Spanish: in the traditional lyric, as in the work of modern Spanish poets, it has connotations of beauty and colour, life and fulfilment, continuity and fecundity; it is sometimes given as a love-token, and its blossom is carried by the bride. Other trees sheltering the lovers are the willow, the holm-oak, the poplar and the pine; other flowers associated with love-making are the poppy and the mallow. The clover, whose leaf is a variant, like the fleur-de-lys and the three legs of Man, of an ancient symbol of maleness, is associated particularly with the feast of St. John, originally a fertility celebration at the summer solstice, and still popularly accepted as the time to seek a lover; gathering clover is an accompaniment to the erotic activity proper to the season.

The thorn in one case is an overt phallic symbol, its wound the wound of love. The planting of a fig-tree is linked with love-making, and its fruiting with the possible consequences. Some of the finest tree symbols also involve the wind: man and woman are two olives hanging together on the same tree, moved rhythmically by the wind; the poplar bends in the wind, swayed by a huge, incomprehensible force, as is the girl by her love.

63

> Bailemos nos ia todas tres, ¡ay! amigas,
> so aquestas avelaneyras frolidas;
> e quen for velida como nos, velidas,
> se amigo amar,
> 5 so aquestas avelaneyras frolidas
> verra baylar.

Bailemos nos ia todas tres, ¡ay! irmanas,
so aqueste ramo destas avelanas;
e quen for louçana como nos, louçanas,
10   se amigo amar,
so aqueste ramo destas avelanas
verra baylar.

Por Deus, ¡ay! amigas, mentr' al non fazemos,
so aqueste ramo frolido bailemos;
15   e quen ben parecer, como nos parecemos,
se amigo amar,
so aqueste ramo, so que nos bailemos,
verra baylar.

Ayras Nunes (*CBN*, No. 818).

l. 2, *so*, 'under'; *avelaneyras frolidas*, 'flowering hazel-groves'; l. 3, *quen for velida*, 'whoever is comely'; l. 4, *se amigo amar*, 'if she loves a lover'; l. 6, *verra*, 'will come'; l. 9, *louçana*, 'youthful and lively'; l. 13, *mentr' al non fazemos*, 'while we are not doing anything else'; l. 15, *quen ben parecer*, 'whoever is good-looking '.

64

Niña y viña,
peral y habar,
malo es de guardar.

Levantéme, oh madre,
5   mañanica frida;
fui a cortar la rosa,
la rosa florida.
Malo es de guardar.

Levantéme, oh madre,
10   mañanica clara;
fui cortar la rosa,
la rosa granada.
Malo es de guardar.

Viñadero malo
15 prenda me pedía;
dile yo un cordone,
dile yo mi cinta.
Malo es de guardar.

Viñadero malo
20 prenda me demanda;
dile yo un [cordone,
dile yo una banda.
Malo es de guardar.]

C. Colombina, fol. 72ᵛ.

l. 5, *frida*, 'cold'.

65

Dentro en el vergel
moriré;
dentro en el rosal
matar m'han.

5 Yo m'iba, mi madre,
las rosas coger;
hallé mis amores
dentro en el vergel.
Dentro en el rosal
10 matar m'han.

CMP, No. 366.

66

Aquellas sierras, madre,
altas son de subir;
corrían los caños,
daban en el torongil.

5 Madre, aquellas sierras
llenas son de flores;
encima d'ellas
tengo mis amores.
Corrían los caños,
10 daban en el torongil.

Diego Pisador, *Libro de música*, 1552
(text from Alín, No. 377).

67

Mimbrera, amigo,
so la mimbrereta.

Y los dos amigos
idos se son, idos,
5 so los verdes pinos,
so la mimbrereta.
Mimbrera, amigo,
so la mimbrereta.

Y los dos amados
10 idos se son ambos,
so los verdes prados,
so la mimbrereta.
Mimbrera, amigo,
so la mimbrereta.

Lope de Rueda, *Auto de Naval y Abigail*,
ca. 1559 (text, slightly adapted, from
Antología, No. 400).

l. 2, *so*, 'under, below'.

68

Ya florecen los árboles, Juan;
mala seré de guardar.

Ya florecen los almendros
y los amores con ellos, Juan;
5   mala seré de guardar.
Ya florecen los árboles, Juan;
mala seré de guardar.

Vásquez, *Recopilación*, II, 14.

69

Daba el sol en los álamos, madre,
y a su sombra me recosté;
dormí, y cuando desperté,
no daba el sol, sino el aire.

Libro de tonos castellanos (late sixteenth
century) (text from Alín, No. 807).

70

De los álamos vengo, madre,
de ver como los menea el ayre.

De los álamos de Sevilla,
de ver a mi linda amiga;
5   de ver como los menea el ayre.
De los álamos vengo, madre,
de ver como los menea el ayre.

Vásquez, *Recopilación*, II, 13.

Cf. this song from Morocco, collected in the mid-twentieth century: En los tálamos
de Sevilla / anda la novia en camisa. / Anday quedo. / En los tálamos de Granada /
anda la novia en delgada. / Anday quedo. (Frenk Alatorre, 'Supervivencias', No. 24.)

71

A aquel árbol que vuelve la foxa
algo se le antoxa.

Aquel árbol del bel mirar
face de maniera flores quiere dar:
5   algo se le antoxa.

Aquel árbol del bel veyer
face de maniera quiere florecer:
algo se le antoxa.

Face de maniera flores quiere dar.
10 Ya se demuestra; salidlas mirar:
algo se le antoxa.

Face de maniera quiere florecer.
Ya se demuestra; salidlas a ver:
algo se le antoxa.

15 Ya se demuestra; salidlas mirar.
Vengan las damas las fructas cortar:
algo se le antoxa.

Ya se demuestra; salidlas a ver.
Vengan las damas la fruta coxer:
20 algo se le antoxa.

El Almirante Don Diego Hurtado de
Mendoza (from the fifteenth-century
Cancionero de Palacio, ed. F. Vendrell,
Madrid, 1945, p. 137).

l. 1, *foxa*, 'leaf'.

72

¡Ay, mezquina,
que se me hincó una espina!
¡Desdichada,
que temo quedar preñada!

MS. 17,698, No. 76.

73

Meu naranjedo no ten fruta,
mas agora ben;
no me lo toque ninguén.

Meu naranjedo florido
5   el fruto no l'es venido,
mas agora ben;
no me lo toque ninguén.

Meu naranjedo granado,
el fruto no l'es llegado,
10   mas agora ben;
no me lo toque ninguén.

CMP, No. 310.

l. 1, *no ten*, 'has no'; l. 2, *ben*, 'it is coming'; l. 3, *ninguén*, 'no one'.
For other lyrics involving the orange, see pp. 4–6, 84. For a sensitive and penetrating examination of the symbolism of the orange, see Reckert, chapter II.

74

Arribica, arribica
de un verde sauze
luchava la niña
con su adorante.

'Romancerillos', No. 52.

75

Alta estaba la peña,
nace la malva en ella.

Alta estaba la peña
riberas del río;
5   nace la malva en ella,
y el trébol florido.

C. Upsala, No. XIX.

76

¡Qué tomillexo,
i qué tomillar!
¡Qué tomillexo
tan malo de arrancar!

Correas, *Arte*, p. 446.

Cf. this twentieth-century oral version from the province of Madrid: ¡Ay, qué tomillito, / ay, qué tomillar! / Ah, qué suavecito / que está de arrancar! (Frenk Alatorre, 'Supervivencias', No. 47).

77
Como se menea la aceituna sevillana,
así se menea tu cuerpecito, serrana.

Agua menudita llueve,
¡cómo escorren las canales!
5   y ábreme la puerta, cielo,
que soy aquél que tu sabes.

Como se menea la aceituna en el olivo,
así se menea tu cuerpecito y el mío.

Navalonguilla, Ávila (Schindler, No. 121).

78
A tu ventana
ha nacido un arbolillo
de la noche a la mañana,
y a tu balcón he de plantar una higuera,
5   que lleguen las ramas a tu cabecera;
y a los nueve meses maduren las brevas,
y a los nueve meses puedes comer de ellas.

Bocigas de Perales (?), Soria (Schindler, No. 592).

79
Prometió mi madre
de no me dar marido
hasta que el perejil
estuviese nacido.

Correas, *Vocabulario*.

Cf. this oral version from Santervás del Burgo, Soria: Dice mi madre / que no me da marido / mientras el cardo / no esté florido. / Yo digo: ¿Cuándo, / cuándo estará florido, / madre, aquel cardo, / madre, aquel cardo? (Schindler, No. 821.)

80

Como flores de almendro
fueron mis bienes,
que nacieron temprano
para perderse.

Foulché-Delbosc, 'Séguedilles', No. 41.

81

Arriméime a un pinu verde
pur ver si me cunsulaba;
ya el pinu cumu era verde,
de verme churar, churaba.

León (Álvarez, p. 86).

l. 3, *ya*, 'and'; l. 4, *churar*, 'to weep'.
See Torner, *Lírica*, No. 36 for many oral variants.

82

Tu cabello y el mío
se han enredado
como las zarzamoras
por los vallados.

Andalucía (Molina, p. 104).

83

Trébole, ¡ay Jesús, cómo huele!
Trébole, ¡ay Jesús, qué olor!

Trébole de la niña virgo
que tenía amores cinco,
encelados y escondidos,
sin gozar de algún favor.
Trébole, ¡ay Jesús, cómo huele!
Trébole, ¡ay Jesús, qué olor!

'Romancerillos', No. 89.

Torner, *Lírica*, No. 1, gives several Golden Age variants.

84

Van por el trébole, trébole van,
van por el trébole al arrabal.
Las mocitas de Ciudad Rodrigo
van por el trébole florido.

Ciudad Rodrigo, Salamanca (Torner,
Lírica, No. 1).

See also No. 199, below.

85

A la rosa del campo
la dijo el lirio;
— Quien pudiera esta noche
dormir contigo.

Castile (Torner, *Lírica*, No. 123).

Torner gives other oral examples including this wedding-song from Salamanca:
Llena va la calle / de rosas y lirios; / llena va la calle / de primas y primos. / Llena va
la calle / de lirios y rosas; / llena va la calle / de mozos y mozas.

Animals and birds

Birds, often diminutive and unspecified, commonly act as lovers'
messengers, as symbols of freedom, or as links with the exile's homeland.
A more precise and vivid usage is that of the imagery of falconry:
love-making again is a death; the man is the hawk or falcon, the woman
the quarry, often the heron. In the Middle Ages and Golden Age, when
the hawk mantling and panting over its prey was a sight familiar to
countryman and courtier alike, such imagery would have an immediacy
which it has now largely lost. The only large animal to appear with any
frequency is the deer. The stag is particularly common in the *gallego*
lyric, often linked with the girl's visit to the river. The wounded hind,
less common, is the girl herself, love again being a hunt and a killing.

Sheep, cows and geese are there merely to be guarded, a natural part
of the rural scene, acting occasionally as confidants. The snail is sometimes associated with the phallic image of the *cuerno*, or with cuckoldry,
but the bull, strangely, is only rarely found with these connotations,
although there are many local songs to accompany the bull-fights in

village festivals (see Torner, *Lírica*, No. 138). Sexual *double-entendres* involving small animals and birds are found in Golden Age *seguidillas*, but these are mostly poor things, of puny and sniggering humour.

86

En as verdes ervas
vi anda' las cervas,
meu amigo.

En os verdes prados
5   vi os cervos bravos,
meu amigo.

E, con sabor d'elhas,
lavey mhas garcetas,
meu amigo.

10   E, con sabor d'elhos,
lavey meus cabelos,
meu amigo.

Des que los lavey,
d'ouro los liey,
15   meu amigo.

Des que las lavara,
d'ouro las liara,
meu amigo.

D'ouro los liey,
20   e vos asperey,
meu amigo.

D'ouro las liara,
e vos asperava,
meu amigo.

Pero Meõgo (*CBN*, No. 1137).

l. 1, *as*, 'the'; *ervas*, 'grass'; l. 4, *os*, 'the'; l. 8, *garcetas*, 'hair (worn hanging down the cheeks)'; l. 13, *Des que los lavey*, 'after I had washed them'; l. 14, *d'ouro los liey*, 'I bound them with gold'; l. 20, *vos asperey*, 'I waited for you'.

87

El ciervo viene herido
de la yerba del amor;
caza tiene el pecador.

C. sevillano, fol. 82.

88

¡Ya va la cierva herida,
ola há,
quedá, quedá, quedá!

MS. 17,698, No. 2.

89

Házeme cosquillas
un ratonzuelo,
y assí toda la noche
paso riendo.

Foulché-Delbosc, 'Séguedilles', No. 233.

90

Una donzelluela
de garbo y pico
ha metido en su jaula
mi pajarico.

Foulché-Delbosc, 'Séguedilles', No. 240.

l. 2, *de garbo y pico*, 'attractive and talkative'.

91

Guíseme caracoles,
señora madre,
qu'el caldillo del cuerno
bueno me sabe.

Foulché-Delbosc, 'Séguedilles', No. 211.

92

Como se menean as troitas no río,
así se menea teu corpo frolido.
Como se menean as troitas na-y auga,
así se menea teu corpo, salada.

Galicia (Torner, Lírica, No. 258).

l. 1, *as troitas*, 'the trout'; *no río*, 'in the river'; l. 2, *corpo*, 'body'; l. 3, *na-y auga*, 'in the water'.

93

¡Válgame Dios, que los ánsares vuelan!
¡Válgame Dios, que saben volar!

Obras de Francisco de Trillo y Figueroa,
ed. A. Gallego Morell, Madrid, 1951,
p. 125.

94

Águila que vas volando,
lleva en el pico estas flores;
dáselas a mis amores,
dile como estoy penando.

Juan de Timoneda, Sarao de amor, 1561,
fol. 13 (text from Alín, No. 462).

95

Arrullaba la tórtola, madre,
por debajo del verde limón;
con el pico derriba la hoja,
con las alas quebranta la flor.

Hoyocasero, Ávila (Torner, Lírica, No. 40).

The same section in Torner contains many other similar lyrics, including this version from Luis de Briceño, *Método de guitarra*, 1626: Bolava la palomita / por encima del verde limón; / con las alas aparta las ramas, / con el pico lleva la flor.

96

Garza del gentil mirar,
cierto cazarte querría
a tu voluntad y mía.

Juan de Timoneda, *Sarao de amor*, 1561,
fol. 32ᵛ (text from Alín, No. 472).

97

Mal ferida va la garça.
Sola va y gritos daba.

Ribericas de aquel río,
donde la garça haze su nido,
5   sola va y gritos daba.

Diego Pisador, *Libro de música*, 1552 (text
from Alín, No. 224).

98

A mi seguem os dous açores;
hum delles morirá d'amores.

Dous açores qu'eu havía,
aquí andam nesta bailía;
5   hum delles morirá d'amores.

Gil Vicente, *Tragicomedia pastoril da
Serra da Estrela*, *Obras completas*,
Vol. IV, p. 197.

l. 1, *seguem*, 'are following'; *os dous açores*, 'the two goshawks'; l. 2, *hum delles*,
'one of them'; l. 4, *nesta bailía*, 'in this dance'.

99

Si tantos halcones
la garza combaten,
por Dios que la maten.

La garza se queja
5   de ver su ventura,

que nunca la deja
gozar del altura.
Con gozo y tristura
la garza combaten;
10 por Dios que la maten.

Luis de Narváez, *Los seis libros del
Delphin de Música*, 1538, ed. E. Pujol,
Barcelona, 1945, No. 39.

100

Montesina era la garza,
y de muy alto volar;
no hay quien la pueda tomar.

Juan del Encina, *Cancionero*, 1496 (text
from *Antología*, No. 348).

The sea

Many of the Galician *cantigas de amigo* have coastal settings, often
localized, and one can sometimes read into the sea motif associations
similar to those of the *baños de amor*. In some of the later Castilian
lyrics, the sea-shore is a setting and resort for the lonely misery of love;
the impersonal vastness of the sea, described briefly and wonderingly
in the tiny lyric, heightens the sense of being dwarfed and helpless before
emotions and situations beyond control, the hypnotic attraction of the
breaking waves and the green deep providing no sympathy in grief, but
only a possible escape from it (see the lyric *Miraba la mar*, p. 21).
The link between sadness and the sea is strengthened by the image of
the *mar de lágrimas*, which is present in the early Mozarabic lyric (see
the *kharja* of Part II, Section A), and survives in the modern oral
tradition.

101

Quantas sabedes amar amigo,
treydes comig' a lo mar de Vigo,
e banharnos-emos nas ondas.

Quantas sabedes amar amado,
5   treydes vos migo ao mar levado,
e banharnos-emos nas ondas.

Treydes comigo ao mar de Vigo,
e veeremo lo meu amigo,
e banharnos-emos nas ondas.

10 Treydes migo a lo mar levado,
e veeremo lo meu amado,
e banharnos-emos nas ondas.

Martin Codax (*CBN*, No. 1231).

l. 2, *treydes comig'*, 'come with me'; l. 3, *banharnos-emos*, 'we will bathe'; l. 5, *migo*, 'with me'; *ao mar levado*, 'to the rough sea' (or perhaps 'to the sea at the flood').

102

Por la mar abajo
van los mis ojos.
Quiero m'ir con ellos,
no vayan solos.

MS. 3915, fol. 319ᵛ.

103

¡Hola, que me lleva la ola,
ola, que me lleva la mar!

C. sevillano, fol. 45ᵛ.

104

Aguas de la mar,
miedo he
que en vosotras moriré.

Ondas turbias, saladas,
5   al mejor de mi dormir

ensueño que me ha de venir
por vosotras, malas hadas;
mil veces os he ensoñadas.
Miedo he
10   que en vosotras moriré.

> Luis Milán, *Libro de música de vihuela de
> mano intitulado El Maestro*, 1535 (text
> from *Antología*, No. 372).

l. 6, *ensueño*, 'I dream'; l. 8, *os he ensoñadas*, 'I have dreamed of you'.

105

Parezen mis penas
olas del mar,
porque vienen unas
cuando otras se van.

> Foulché-Delbosc, 'Séguedilles', No. 142.

Cf. this oral example from Argentina: Mis dichas y mis desdichas / son cual las olas
del mar: / mis desdichas las que vienen, / mis dichas las que se van (Torner, *Lírica*, No.
131).

106

Las ondas de la mar,
¡cuán menudicas van!

> H. González de Eslava, *Ensalada de la
> Flota* (late sixteenth century) (text from
> *Antología*, No. 264).

107

A la mar fui por naranjas,
cosa que la mar no tiene;
toda vine mojadita
de olas que van y vienen.

> Asturias (Torner, *Lírica*, No. 150).

108

A la mar fueron mis ojos
a por agua pa llorar;
y se han venido sin ella,
que se ha secado la mar.

Torrejoncillo, Cáceres (Schindler, No. 383).

l. 2, *pa*, a colloquial form of *para*.

The ship

The ship motif is commonly linked with the lover's departure (see,
for example, *Per ribeyra do rio*, p. 35); often he has no choice, being
pressed into the king's service or imprisoned in the galleys. In other
poems, however, there is a perception of the beauty of ship and sea
together, a passive joy in the marine rhythms and the movement of
the vessel. The small ferryboat has a pleasant and appreciated role in
bringing the lovers together.

109

Vi los barcos, madre,
vilos y no me valen.

C. Upsala, No. XXVIII.

110

Alcé los ojos,
miré la mar,
vi a mis amores
a la vela andar.

MS. 17,698, No. 149.

111

Vaste, amore;
¡quién fuera agora el remador!
Amor, y vaste;
¡quién fuera agora el que remase!

MS. 17,698, No. 11.

112

Salen de Sevilla
barquetes nuevos,
que de verde aya
llevan los remos.

'Romancerillos', No. 79.

113

Tocan los clarines
al alborada;
los remos se mueven,
retumba el agua.

Lope de Vega, Las bodas entre el alma y el
amor divino, Obras, Vol. II, p. 32.

114

¡Cómo retumban los remos,
madre, en el agua,
con el fresco viento
de la mañana!

Lope de Vega, Entremés del soldadillo,
Obras, Vol. II, p. 175.

115

Salen las galeras
de el puerto, madre,
con las velas tendidas
y en popa el aire.

5 Y por ver cómo reman
subí a la popa;
con el son de los remos
dormíme toda.

Foulché-Delbosc, 'Séguedilles', Nos. 32–33.

116
Oi se parte la carabela;
mi corazón en prisiones queda.

MS. 17,698, No. 149.

117
Salen de Sanlúcar,
rompiendo el agua,
a la Torre del Oro
barcos de plata.

Foulché-Delbosc, 'Séguedilles', p. 309.

118
De tu cama a la mía
pasa un barquillo.
Aventúrate y pasa,
moreno mío.

Foulché-Delbosc, 'Séguedilles', No. 47.

The *molinico de amor*

The association of milling and love-making is international and of long standing. The miller himself, like his Chaucerian archetype, is traditionally 'ful bigge . . . of braun, and eek of bones', and much interested in 'sinne and harlotryes'. Some English folk-songs are mere series of bawdy *double-entendres* based on the machinery and processes of milling (e.g. *Matthew the Miller, The Miller and the Lass*; see James Reeves, *The Idiom of the People*, London, 1958, p. 156, and *The Everlasting Circle*, London, 1960, p. 187). These wearisome mechanical minutiae have no place in the succinct Spanish lyric, but dual meanings of *moler* and *molino* are present in several songs (see also *Solía que andaba*, p. 17).

119

Muele, molinico,
molinico del amor.
— Que no puedo moler, no.

Cancionero de Juan de Molina, 1527, ed. E.
Asensio, Valencia, 1952, p. 49.

120

Molinero sois, amor,
y sois moledor.

Correas, *Vocabulario*.

121

Quítese allá,
señor don Miguel;
apártese allá,
que le enharinaré.

Correas, *Vocabulario*.

A song collected by Schindler (No. 353) in Montehermoso, Cáceres includes the
lines: Y aparte que va, / y apártese usté, / que soy moli-molinera / y le enjarinaré.

122

Vengo de moler, morena,
de los molinos de enfrente.
Duermo con la molinera;
no lo sabe el tío Vicente.
5   Que vengo de moler, morena.

Vengo de moler, morena,
de los molinos de abajo.
Duermo con la molinera;
no me cobra su trabajo.
10   Que vengo de moler, morena.

Vengo de moler, morena,
de los molinos de arriba.
Duermo con la molinera;
no lo sabe el tío Barriga.
15   Que vengo de moler, morena.

Navalonguilla, Ávila (Schindler, No. 120).

Schindler also gives (No. 430) a more euphemistic version from León ('Hablo con la molinera . . .').

No quiero ser monja, no

A conventional theme in the lyric is the girl forced into a nunnery against her will. This is another manifestation of the preoccupation with fertility and the realization of potential. The girl is full of the urges of her incipient womanhood; sometimes these are directed at a particular lover, sometimes they are merely the vaguely comprehended feelings of adolescence. However near fulfilment these urges are, they are stifled by the cloister wall and the black habit of the nun. For a society whose continuance depends on fertility, the girl becomes a symbol of unrealized fecundity, of joyous potential ignored. The implications of her marriage with the Church are for the lyric totally negative. There is evidence that the taking of the veil was not always a bar to sexual activity, and the worldly nun is found in the bawdier kind of medieval literature. There, however, she excites disgust; she is vicious, a living lie. The unwilling novice of the traditional lyric, in contrast, is an innocent, open about her feelings, distressed by the decision of her family to stifle them. The theme of wasted fecundity is nowhere better expressed than in the superb contrasting image of the young breasts under the black habit of No. 126.

123
Agora que soy niña
quiero alegría,
que no se sirve Dios
de mi mongía.

5 Agora que soy niña
   niña en cabello,
   me queréys meter monja
   en el monesterio.
   Que no se sirve Dios
10 de mi mongía.
   Agora que soy niña
   quiero alegría,
   que no se sirve Dios
   de mi mongía.

                    Vásquez, *Recopilación*, II, 12.

124

No quiero ser monja, no,
que niña namoradica só.

Dexadme con mi plazer,
con mi plazer y alegría,
5 dexadme con mi porfía,
que niña mal penadica só.

                    CMP, No. 9.

125

Agora que sé d'amor me metéis monja.
¡Ay, Dios, qué grave cosa!

Agora que sé d'amor de caballero,
agora me metéis monja en el monesterio.
5 ¡Ay, Dios, qué grave cosa!

                    Vásquez, *Recopilación*, I, 10.

126

No me las enseñes más,
que me matarás.

Estábase la monja
en el monesterio,
5 sus teticas blancas
de so el velo negro.
Más,
que me matarás.

Sánchez de Badajoz, *Recopilación*, fol.
CXIII.

l. 6, *de so*, 'under'.
Cf. *C. Upsala*, No. V: No me los amuestres más, / que me matarás. / Son tan lindos
y tan bellos / que a todos matas con ellos; / y aunque yo muero por vellos, / no me
los amuestres más, / que me matarás.

127
¡Mal haya mi padre! que no me casó
con aquel muchacho que quería yo.

Desde pequeñita me fui al convento
con mucha alegría y mucho contento.
5 Pero la alegría pronto se acabó.
¡Mal haya mi padre! que no me casó
con aquel muchacho que quería yo.

Guisando, Ávila (Schindler, No. 75).

128
¿Qué dirán de la freila?
¿Qué dirán della,
si abraza los robles,
pensando que eran hombres?

Correas, *Vocabulario*.

l. 1, *freila*, 'lay sister'.

129
¡Cómo lo tuerce y lava
la monjita el su cabello!
¡Cómo lo tuerce y lava!
Luego lo tiende al hielo.

Foulché-Delbosc, 'Séguedilles', No. 307.

130

Aunque me vedes
morenica en el agua,
no seré yo frayla.

Una madre,
5   que a mí crió,
mucho me quiso
y mal me guardó.
A los pies de mi cama
los canes ató.
10   Atólos ella,
desatélos yo;
metiera, mi madre,
al mi lindo amor.
No seré yo frayla.

15   Una madre,
que a mí criara,
mucho me quiso,
mal me guardara.
A los pies de mi cama
20   los canes atara.
Atólos ella,
yo los desatara,
y metiera, madre,
al que más amaba.
25   No seré yo frayla.

C. galanes, pp. 66–67.

l. 1, *vedes*, 'you see'; l. 3, *frayla*, 'lay sister'.
The poem is unusual both in the type of parallelism it employs and in its fusing of motifs normally separate.

131

En Vistalegre dixin,
baixando a Vilagarcía:

eu monxa non quero ser,
casada . . . ¡non séi qué diga!

Galicia (Torner, *Lírica*, No. 104).

l. 1, *dixin*, 'they say'; l. 2, *baixando*, 'going down'; l. 3, *eu monxa non quero ser*, 'I don't want to be a nun'.

132

Mis padres, por no casarme,
me dan hábito y cordón;
permita Dios, si soy monja,
que muera sin confesión.

Segovia (Torner, *Lírica*, No. 104).

La bella malmaridada

The *malmaridada* or *malcasada* theme, often treated humorously, must reflect a real situation in which, in the restricted marriage market of the village, marriages of true love were outnumbered by those resulting from parental pressure or sheer desperation. The prevailing feminine viewpoint common to most of the traditional lyrics is again dominant: there are no *malcasados* to complain of wifely inadequacies, whereas the lumpish, lazy, sexually inadequate and frequently aged husband is repeatedly the target for complaints and abuse, or the recipient, often dormant, of the horns of cuckoldry. The girl, like the *monja* of the preceding section, is trapped in a situation where her youth, beauty and vitality are robbed of their natural outlet; again we have the preoccupation with fruition and fulfilment, stifled by circumstance.

The potentially unfaithful wife is at the centre of the code of courtly love which dominates medieval court verse, but one need not seek any downward influence of this convention on the *malmaridada* theme. The traditional *malmaridada* poem has its roots in fact rather than in convention, and rings of the true emotion bound up in a situation where refuge from misery must be sought in humour or unfaithfulness. The husband in the courtly code is merely a peripheral shadow, a necessary but featureless reason for the secrecy which is one of the props of the elaborate structure of the code, whereas the husband of the *malmaridada* is all too tiresomely present.

133

Pinguele, respinguete,
¡qué buen San Juan es éste!

Fuése mi marido
a Seo del Arzobispo;
5   dejárame un fijo
y fallóme cinco.
¡Qué buen San Juan es éste!

Dejárame un fijo
y fallóme cinco;
10   dos hube en el Carmen
y dos en San Francisco.
¡Qué buen San Juan es éste!

C. Colombina, fol. 86.

l. 1, *Pinguele, respinguete*, probably just nonsense words; ll. 5–6, *dejárame un fijo* / *y fallóme cinco*, 'he left me with one child, and when he came back I had five'.
Cf. Torner, *Lírica*, No. 148: Vino el mió Xuan de la Habana / tan probe como marchó; / dexárame cuatro fíos / y con siete s'atopó; / dexárame cuatro fíos / y con siete s'atopó; / nunca me dixo el mió Xuan, / Marica, ¿quién te los dió? (Asturias).

134

No querades, fija,
marido tomar
para sospirar.

Fuése mi marido
5   a la frontera;
sola me dexaba
en tierr'agena.
No querades, fija,
marido tomar
10   para sospirar.

CMP, No. 240.

135

Viejo malo en la mi cama,
por mi fe, non dormirá.

Es un viejo desdonado,
no puede comer bocado;
5 él beberá lo cobrado,
toda me gomitará.

Hija, él tiene parientes
muy ricos y muy potentes;
aunque le falten los dientes,
10 así no te morderá.

CMP, No. 455.

l. 3, *desdonado*, 'gross, graceless'; l. 6, *toda me gomitará*, 'he'll be sick all over me'.

136

Soy garridica
y vivo penada
por ser malcasada.

MS. 5593, fol. 82.

137

Mi marido anda cuytado;
yo juraré que está castrado.

Zafra, *Villancicos*.

l. 1, *anda cuytado*, 'has something worrying him'.

138

Abaja los ojos, casada,
no mates a quien te miraba.

Casada, pechos hermosos,
abaja tus ojos graciosos.
5 No mates a quien te miraba,
abaja los ojos, casada.

Vásquez, *Villancicos*, No. 7.

139

Cuando mi padre me casó,
muriera yo.

Pues que me dió
al mal villano,
5   que tarde ni temprano
no sabe, no,
no puede, no,
no acierta, no,
sino'n dormir.
10   ¡O qué morir!
Ay, ay, ay,
que muerta só,
pues que me dió
al mal villano.

Petrus Albertus Vila, *Odarum*, 1571 (text
from Alín, No. 620).

140

A la malcasada
déle Dios plazer,
que la bien casada
no lo a menester.

MS. 3168, fol 43.

141

Todas cantan en la boda,
y la novia llora.

Correas, *Vocabulario*.

142
Entre yo y mi marido
valemos algo,
porque yo soy blanca
y él es cornado.

Correas, *Arte.*

There is a double pun: *blanca* and *cornado* are both names of coins, and *cornado* also means 'cuckolded'.

143
No me case mi madre
con ombre gordo,
que en entrando en la cama
güele a mondongo.

5 No me case mi madre
con ombre grande,
que me sube en el poyo
para besarme.

No me case mi madre
10 con ombre chico,
que le llevo delante
por avanico.

Foulché-Delbosc, 'Séguedilles', Nos. 94–96.

l. 4, *güele*, 'he smells'; *mondongo*, 'guts'.

144
No me vengas más a ver
con tu yegua Reluciente,
que el potro de mi marío
relincha cuando la siente.

Molina, p. 143.

145

Estaba la molinera
sentadita en su molino,
contando cuatro pesetas
para una fanega de trigo.

5　Molinera, molinera,
¡Qué descolorida estás!
Desde el día de la boda
no has dejado de llorar.

No has dejado de llorar,
10　ni tampoco de sentir.
Molinera, molinera,
de pena vas a morir.

Montehermoso, Cáceres (Schindler,
No. 359).

146

Bésame y abráçame,
marido mío,
y daros [hé] en la mañana
camisón limpio.

5　Yo nunca vi hombre
vivo estar tan muerto,
ni hazer el dormido
estando despierto.
Andad, marido, alerta,
10　y tened brío,
y daros [hé] en la mañana
camisón limpio.

C. Upsala, No. XVIII.

l. 3, *daros* [*hé*], 'I shall give you'.

Yo me soy la morenica

The motif of the little dark girl is dual and paradoxical. There are numerous lyrics expressing the admiration or love of a man for a *morenica*, in which the girl is seen as attractive and desirable, but in the many poems expressing the girl's own feelings, to be *morena* is hateful, the mark of the peasant, the inevitable consequence of watching her flock or mowing the hay in the Spanish sun. Her beauty is destroyed, the men will not look at her. The girl's complaints, therefore, relate to darkness of skin; the man's praise is of the black hair and dark eyes which, set off by a pale complexion, are traditional features of the Spanish concept of beauty. There is also a link with the *aire de amores*: to be burned by the wind is to lose one's virginity and hence to be less desirable; the *morena*, therefore, is a woman, in contrast to the pure, virginal *blanca* (see Nos. 52, 59).

147
Los cabellos negros,
la niña blanca:
entre nubes negras
parece el alba.

MS. 3890, fol. 103ᵛ.

148
— Digas, morena garrida,
¿cuándo serás mi amiga?
— Cuando esté florida la peña
d'una flor morena.

Petrus Albertus Vila, *Odarum*, 1571 (text from Alín, No. 621).

l. 1, *garrida*, 'fine, bonny'.

149
Cuando mi morenita
su cuerpo baña,
sírvele de espejo
el cristal del agua.

'Romancerillos', No. 52.

150
Si tienes las piernas
como la cara,
tú eres la morenita
que yo buscaba.

'Romancerillos', No. 52.

151
Morenita me llaman, madre,
desde el día en que nací,
y el galán que me ronda la puerta
blanca y rubia le parecí.

'Romancerillos', No. 71.

152
Criéme en la aldea,
híceme morena;
si en villa me criara
más bonica fuera.

C. Horozco, p. 108.

153
Aunque soi morena,
blanca io nací;
guardando el ganado
la color perdí.

MS. 3915, fol. 320.

The poem survives among the Sephardic Jews: Morenika mi yama, / yo blanka nasí, / di pasear galana / mi kolor perdí. (Frenk Alatorre, 'Supervivencias', No. 42.)

154
¡No me llaméys sega la erva,
sino morena!

Un amigo que yo avía
sega la erva me dezía.
5   ¡No me llaméys sega la erva,
sino morena!

Vásquez, *Recopilación*, II, 43.

l. 1, *sega la erva*, 'cut-the-grass'.

155

Morenica m'era yo;
dizen que sí, dizen que no.

Unos que bien me quieren
dizen que sí;
5   otros que por mí mueren
dizen que no.
Morenica m'era yo;
dizen que sí, dizen que no.

Vásquez, *Recopilación*, I, 8.

156

Aunque soi morenita un poco,
no me doi nada;
con el agua del almendruco
me lavo la cara.

Foulché-Delbosc, 'Séguedilles', No. 298.

According to Covarrubias, the *almendruco*, or green almond, was a 'golosina de preñadas' (*Tesoro de la lengua castellana*, ed. Riquer, Barcelona, 1943, p. 96).

157

Déixame ir que vou de presa,
que vou coller a berbena,
que quero lavar a cara,
que me chamaron morena.

Galicia (Torner, *Lírica*, No. 157).

l. 1, *Déixame ir*, 'Let me go'; *vou de presa*, 'I'm in a hurry'; l. 2, *vou coller a berbena*, 'I'm going to gather the vervain'; l. 3, *a*, 'the' (here 'my'); l. 4, *chamaron*, 'they called'. For other oral *morenita* lyrics, see Torner, *Lírica*, No. 157.

The *serrana*

The Spanish *serrana* poem is not, as used to be thought in the days
when the dominant French criticism saw every road in the lyric as
leading from France, a mere coarse imitation of the *pastourelle*. The
genres have in common the encounter of opposites: male with female;
noble with peasant; urbane experience with untravelled naïvety. The
serrana, however, has definite characteristics of its own: the harshness
of landscape and climate; the request to the girl for succour or direction;
the aggressiveness of the girl; an occasional tendency towards coarseness
(most in evidence in the *serranas* of the *Libro de Buen Amor*). It is now
generally accepted that the *serrana* is a native peninsular strain of an
international family to which the *pastourelle* also belongs, though this
is not to deny that well-read writers of *serrana* poems, such as Santillana
and Gil Vicente, may have been familiar with both traditions.

158

Paséisme aor'allá, serrana,
que no muera yo en esta montaña.

Paséisme aor'allende el río,
que estoy triste, mal herido,
5   que no muera yo en esta montaña.

CMP, No. 244 (attributed to Escobar).

159

Encima del puerto
vide una serrana,
sin duda es galana.

Encima del puerto,
5   allá cerca el río,
vide una serrana
del cuerpo garrido;
sin duda es galana.

Encima del puerto,
10   allá cerca el vado,
vide una serrana
del cuerpo lozano;
sin duda es galana.

C. galanes, pp. 64–65.

l. 2, *vide*, 'I saw'; l. 7, *garrido*, 'fine, comely'.

160

¡Sañosa está la niña!
¡Ay Dios!, ¿quién le hablaría?

En la sierra anda la niña
su ganado a repastar;
5   hermosa como las flores,
sañosa como la mar.
Sañosa como la mar
está la niña.
¡Ay Dios!, ¿quién le hablaría?

Gil Vicente, *Auto da Sibila Casandra, Obras
completas*, Vol. I, p. 62 (with
modifications from *Antología*, No. 353).

161

¿Por dó pasaré la sierra,
gentil serrana morena?

Tu ru ru ru lá:
¿quién la pasará?
5   Tu ru ru ru rú:
no la pases tú.
Tu ru ru ru ré:
yo la pasaré.
Dí, serrana, por tu fe,
10   si naciste en esta tierra,
¿por dó pasaré la sierra,
gentil serrana morena?

Ti ri ri ri rí:
queda tú aquí.
15 Tu ru ru ru rú:
¿qué más quieres tú?
To ro ro ro ró:
que yo sola estó.
Serrana, no puedo, no,
20 que otro amor me da guerra.
¿Cómo pasaré la sierra,
gentil serrana morena?

Gil Vicente, *Triunfo do Inverno, Obras completas*, Vol. IV, pp. 279–80.

l. 1, ¿Por dó . . . ?, 'Which way . . . ?'

162
¡Hávalas, hávalas, hala,
hava la frol y la gala!

Allá arriba, arriba,
junto a mi logare,
5 viera yo serranas
cantar y bailare;
y entre todas ellas
mi linda zagala;
¡hava la frol y la gala!

C. Horozco, p. 166.

ll. 1–2, *¡Háva . . . !*, 'Hurrah for . . . !'; l. 2, *frol*, 'flower'; l. 4, *logare*, 'village';
l. 6, *bailare*, 'to dance'; the source has the odd form *baxlare* (perhaps a mistake for *baylare*).

163
Caracoles la niña lavaba.
Serranita, tus pechos me agradan.
Lava uno y saliban dos,
lava uno y saliban dos;
5 que ni uno ni dos ni nada;

serranita, de pies en el agua.
Lavan tres y saliban cuatro,
lavan tres y saliban cuatro;
que ni cuatro ni tres ni dos ni uno ni nada;
10   descalcita, de pies en el agua;
serranita, tus pechos me agradan.

Santorcaz, Madrid (Schindler, No. 480).

l. 3, etc., *saliban*, an archaic or vulgar form of *salían*.

164

El puerto de Guadarrama
no sé si lo pasaré;
si le paso o no le paso,
eso sí que no lo sé;
5   si le paso o no le paso,
dime, morena, ¿qué haré?

Asturias (Torner, *Lírica*, No. 97).

165

¡Ay de mí! perdí el camino
en esta triste montaña.
Déxame meté'l rebañu,
pastora, en la to cabaña.

5   Entre la espesa nublina,
¡ay de mí! perdí el camino;
déxame pasar la noche
en la cabaña contigo.

Asturias (Torner, 'Indice', No. 38).

l. 4, *la to*, 'your'; l. 5, *nublina*, 'mist'.

The *pastorcico*

The shepherd-boy, newly arrived, is often an object of interest,
occasionally a threat, for the girl in the lyric. The situation is a
commonplace of rural life: the herdsman, especially under the Spanish

transhumance system, travels around much more than the ploughman; he is often footloose and carefree, and usually eager for company and conversation.

166

Llueve menudico
y hace la noche oscura;
el pastorcico es nuevo,
no iré segura.

Jaime de Huete, Vidriana, 1530 (text from
Alín, No. 142).

167

¡Fuera, fuera, fuera,
el pastorcico!
Que en el campo dormirás
y no comigo.

Juan de Timoneda, Sarao de amor, 1561,
fol. 54 (text from Alín, No. 473).

168

Si el pastorcico es nuevo
y anda enamorado,
si se descuida y duerme,
¿quién guardará el ganado?
5 Digas, el pastorcico,
galán y tan pulido,
¿cúyas eran las vacas
que pastan par del río?
— Vuestras son, mi señora,
10 y mío es el suspiro.
Si se descuida y duerme,
¿quién guardará el ganado?

Vásquez, Recopilación, II, 1.

l. 8, *par del*, 'beside the'.
Cf. No. 170.

169

Pastorcico nuevo,
de color de amor,
no sois vos, vida mía,
pa labrador.

MS. 3168, fol. 44.

l. 4, *pa*, a colloquial form of *para*.
The poem is also found in MS. 3915, fol. 66ᵛ. (l. 2: 'de color de açor').

170

Las ovejitas, madre,
pasan el río,
y el pastor con las damas
entretenido.

5   ¿Quién las cuidará, madre,
quién las cuidará?
Que las cuide quien quiera,
para mí ya, ya.

Asturias (Torner, 'Indice', No. 99).

Woman's work

Mention has been made in the Introduction of the link between
the female village gathering and the feminine viewpoint dominant in
the lyric. Certain songs in each village may be partly reserved by habit
to accompany specific activities, such as washing clothes in the river,
though there need be no overt link of subject-matter with activity.
Many songs, however, do mention certain female occupations, particularly
spinning, whereas relatively few make any allusion to ploughing, sowing
or other specifically male activities. The woman too idle to spin is the
subject of several lyrics.

171

El lunes hay que barrer,
el martes hay que fregar,
el miércoles al molino
para el jueves amasar,
5   el viernes hacer colada
para el sábado lavar,
y el domingo, como es fiesta,
no se puede trabajar.

¿Que cuándo vas a hilar, hilar, María,
10 que cuándo vas a hilar, hilar, hilar,
que cuándo vas a hilar, hilar, María?
— Mañanita de San Juan.

Asturias (Torner, *Lírica*, No. 124).

172

Cuando veo la rueca,
de mío caigo muerta;
cuando veo el lino,
me fino.

Correas, *Vocabulario*.

l. 2, *de mío*, 'on my own, without any help'.

173

Cásate cunmigu Xiuan,
que soy buena filadora:
cada día filu un filu,
cada mes, una mazorga.

León (Álvarez, p. 142).

l. 1, *Xiuan*, a Leonese form of *Juan*; l. 2, *buena filadora*, 'good at spinning'; l. 3, *filu un filu*, 'I spin a thread'; l. 4, *mazorga*, 'spindleful'.

174
Rueca ruxidera,
moza durmidera:
la rueca, ruxir,
la moza, durmir.

León (Álvarez, p. 143).

l. 1, *ruxidera*, 'whirring'; l. 3, *ruxir*, 'to whirr'.

175
Hilanderas, ¿qué hicisteis o hilasteis,
si en marzo no curasteis?
Fuí al mar, vine del mar,
hice casa sin hogar,
5   sin azada ni azadón,
y sin ayuda de varón;
chirrizchizchiz.

Correas, *Vocabulario*.

Correas explains this as the 'dicho y canto de la golondrina, reprendiendo a las descuidadas, habiendo ella tanto hecho'.

176
Que non sé filar
ni aspar ni devanar.

Y mercóme mi marido
un arrova de lino
5   que los perros y los gatos
en ella fazían nido.

Que non sé filar
ni aspar ni devanar.

C. Colombina, fol. 100ᵛ.

l. 1, *filar*, 'to spin'; l. 3, *mercó*, 'bought'.

177

La rueca perdí,
el fuso non fallo;
tres días hay
que lo ando buscando.

Asturias (Torner, Lírica, No. 124).

l. 2, *fuso*, 'spindle'; *non fallo*, 'I can't find'.
Cf. Correas, *Vocabulario*: Perdí la rueca / y el huso no hallo; / tres días ha / que le ando en el rastro.

Seasons and festivals

Some of the songs associated with Christmas and Easter have a literate air and a complication of syntax over-riding the limitations of line and stanza, and are evidently not of popular origin, though there are many exceptions to this. There is usually, however, a greater feeling of spontaneity, of natural association between the genre and the season celebrated, in the many lyrics connected with the feast of St. John (June 24th). The official christianization of the midsummer solstice has not usurped in Spain its celebration as a festival of fertility and particularly as a time for finding a lover; picking the *trébol* is associated particularly with the feast of St. John; other activities suitable to the season are walking in the dew and bathing with one's lover. Another celebration with clearly pre-Christian roots is that of the coming of May, the warming of the earth and the springing of new life. There are numerous songs of the cereal harvest, many of which refer to and were sung by the temporarily migrant *segadores*, and another considerable group is associated with olive-gathering; this is one of the few activities in the agricultural cycle involving male and female participation, and the olive-grove at the time of *recolección* is therefore thought of as a place to find a lover.

Christmas and Easter

178

Brincan y bailan los peces en el río,
brincan y bailan de ver a Dios nacido.
Brincan y bailan los peces en el agua,
brincan y bailan de ver nacida el alba.

5 En el portal de Belén
    nació un clavel encarnado
    que por redimir al mundo
    se ha vuelto lirio morado.

    Brincan y bailan los peces . . .

                Burgos (Torner, 'Indice', No. 192).

179
    ¡Quedito, quedo,
    quedo, pastor!
    llega con tiento
    a la más bella flor;
5 suspende el aliento,
    suprime la voz,
    que duerme mi Niño,
    que duerme mi Dios.

            Cejador, No. 1069 (seventeenth century).

180
    Tortolilla, que llevas
    pajas al nido,
    en Belén las recoja
    tu dulce pico,
5 y lleguen tus alas
    quedito, pasito,
    y en los blandos acentos
    tus tiernos gemidos,
    quedito, pasito,
10 arrullen al niño
    que llora dormido.

            Cejador, No. 1111 (seventeenth century).

181
    Venida es, venida,
    al mundo la vida.

            Álvarez Gato, p. 153.

182

Esta noche es Nochebuena,
y mañana Navidad,
que está la Virgen de parto
y a las doce parirá.

5 Yo te regalo un cordero,
lo mejor de mi ganado,
pa que sepas que te quiero,
pa que sepas que te amo.

Esta noche ha de nacer
10 el señor de los señores;
y esta noche ha de nacer
como un ramito de flores.

Esta noche los pastores
se quedan en el olvido,
15 tocando las castañuelas
y haciendo fiestas al niño.

Santorcaz, Madrid (Schindler, No. 481).

ll. 7–8, *pa*, a colloquial form of *para*.

183

Madre, a la puerta hay un niño,
más hermoso que el sol bello,
y dice que tiene frío.
— Pues díle que entre, se calentará,
5 porque en este pueblo ya no hay caridad,
y nunca la ha habido ni tampoco la habrá.

Jarandilla, Cáceres (Schindler, No. 312).

184

Alegría,
que ya viene el día.

Burgos (Torner, *Lírica*, No. 13).

Cf. Lope de Vega, *El Cardenal de Belén*: Alegráos, pastores, / ya viene el albore. /
Tened alegría, / que ya viene el día. (*Obras*, Vol. IV, p. 182.)

185

La Virgen lava pañales
y los tiende en el romero,
y los pajaritos cantan
y el agua se va riendo.
5 ¡Ay, ay, ay, portalito gracioso!
¡Ay, ay, ay, qué bonito que estás!

Medinaceli, Soria (Schindler, No. 728).

186

En el portal de Belén
la noche se ha vuelto día,
porque el sol está brillando
entre San José y María.
5 Que toquen la gaita,
que toque el tambor;
alégrese el mundo,
que ha nacido Dios.

En un portal de Belén,
10 llenito de telarañas,
nació el Niño Jesús,
el Redentor de las almas.
Que toquen la gaita . . .

Vozmediano, Soria (Schindler, No. 882).

187

¡Oh qué mañana de Pascua!
¡Oh qué mañana de flores!
¡Oh qué mañana de Pascua
ha amanecido, señores!

5 ¡Ay, qué mañana de Pascua,
Pascua de Resurrección!
Todas las aves del campo
adoraban al Señor.

¡Ay, qué mañana de Pascua,
10 Pascua de grande alegría!
Todas las flores del campo
adoraban a María.

> Navarrevisca, Ávila (Schindler, No. 144,
> with further stanzas).

188
Desque la Pascua vieno
con flores me entretengo.

Día de Pascua era,
dánzalo bien, morena.

5   Día de Pascua, madre,
que prive mi donaire.

Llegó Pascua de flores
con todos los amores.

Llegó Pascua florida,
10 danza con garbo, niña.

> Asturias (Torner, *Cancionero*, No. 159).

l. 1, *Desque*, 'since'; *vieno*, 'came'.

May

189
Las mañanas de abril
dulces son de dormir;
las de mayo mejor,
si no despierta el amor.

> Correas, *Vocabulario*.

Cf. a modern version from Cuenca: Las mañanicas de abril / son muy dulces de dormir; / y las de mayo / sin fin ni cabo. (A. González Palencia and E. Mele, *La maya*, Madrid, 1944, p. 49.)

190

Entra Mayo y sale Abril,
tan garridico le vi venir.

Entra Mayo con sus flores,
sale Abril con sus amores,
5 y los dulces amadores
comiençan a bien servir.

CMP, No. 76.

191

Mañanitas floridas
del mes de mayo,
despertad a mi niña,
no duerma tanto.

'Romancerillos', No. 52.

192

Ya viene mayo, mayo,
mocitas, mozas,
ya viene mayo, mayo,
para nosotras.

5 Ya viene mayo, mayo,
mocitas, mozas,
y arriba resalada
para vosotras.

Ya viene mayo, mayo,
10 ya viene el rumbo,
ya viene la alegría
pa todo el mundo.

Este mayo es de pino,
alto y derecho;
15 se parece a los mozos
que lo han puesto.

Este mayo es de pino,
alto y torcido;
se parece a los mozos
20   que lo han traído.

Montenegro de Cameros, Soria
(Schindler, No. 747).

l. 13, *mayo*, 'maypole'.

193

Ya estamos a treinta
de este abril cumplido:
alegrarse, damas,
que mayo ha venido.

5   Ha venido mayo,
bienvenido sea
para las casadas,
viudas y doncellas.

Murcia (Torner, *Lírica*, No. 110).

San Juan

194

¡Albo diya ešte diya,
diya de l'Anṣara ḥaqqā!
Beštiréy me-w l-mudabbaŷ
wa našuqqu r-rumḥa šaqqā.

García Gómez, No. XXV.

Mozarabic *kharja* of about 1100. The meaning is: 'Bright day this day, / day of the Anṣara [midsummer solstice festival] in truth! / I shall put on my embroidered [tunic] / and we will break the lance together.'

195

San Juan el Verde pasó por aquí;
mas ha de un año que nunca le ví.

Hernán Núñez, *Refranes o proverbios en
romance*, Salamanca, 1555.

196

Mañanita de San Juan
levántate tempranito,
y verás en la ventana
de hierbabuena un ramito.

5   ¡Oh, la niña, la enramada,
en la noche tan serena!
Y la música resuena
en lo profundo del mar.

Candeleda, Ávila (Schindler, No. 57).

197

Caballero, queráysme dexar,
que me dirán mal.

¡Oh, qué mañanica, mañana,
la mañana de San Juan,
5   cuando la niña y el caballero
ambos se yvan a bañar!
Caballero, queráysme dexar,
que me dirán mal.

Vásquez, *Recopilación*, I, 13.

198

Que no cogeré yo berbena
la mañana de sant Juan,
pues mis amores se van.

'Romancerillos', No. 89.

199

¿Cómo quieres que olvide, y habiendo estado
¡y olé, serrana! y habiendo estado
a cortar el trébole, el trébole, el trébole,
a cortar el trébole, la noche de San Juan?

5 Las horas olvidadas contigo hablando
¡y olé, serrana! contigo hablando;
a cortar el trébole, el trébole, el trébole,
a cortar el trébole los mis amores van.

Navarrevisca, Ávila (Schindler, No. 145).

The song is well known in many areas (see Schindler, Nos. 6, 291, 319, etc.). Frenk Alatorre, 'Supervivencias', No. 14, gives a Golden Age version: A coger el trébol, damas, / la mañana de San Juan, / a coger el trébol, damas, / que después no habrá lugar.

200

Mañana de San Juan, mozas,
vamos a coger rosas.

Correas, *Vocabulario*.

201

Mi reina,
¿qué tanto ha que no se peina?
Mi galán,
desde San Juan.

Correas, *Vocabulario*.

202

Vamos a la playa,
noche de San Juan,
que se alegra la tierra,
y retumba el mar.

Foulché-Delbosc, 'Séguedilles', p. 310.

Harvest

203

Esta parva de trigo
vale un tesoro:
paja como la seda,
granos de oro.

Andalucía (Molina, p. 142).

204

Tres horas seguidas
llevo trillando.
No me toque usted el cuerpo,
que está quemando.

Andalucía (Molina, p. 142).

205

A segar son idos
tres con una hoz;
mientras uno siega,
holgaban los dos.

Correas, *Vocabulario*.

This survives in Madrid and La Mancha: A segar, segadores, / tres con una hoz, / mientras el uno siega / descansan los dos. / Descansan los dos, niñas, / descansan los dos, / a segar, segadores, / tres con una hoz. (See Frenk Alatorre, 'Supervivencias', No. 61.)

206

Ya vienen los segadores,
de pan y también de hierba.
Ya vienen los segadores
de cortar la hierbabuena.
5   Y el segador que no canta
por la tarde la tonada,
ha bebido poco vino
o no corta la guadaña.

Navarrevisca, Ávila (Schindler, No. 130).

There are other versions from Arbujuelo, Soria (Schindler, No. 583): De segar de tierra baja / ya vienen los segadores, / y comen pan de centeno, / y beben agua de balsa.; and from Medinaceli, Soria (Schindler, No. 733): Ya vienen los segadores / de segar de la Carpiña, / muertos de hambre, sin dinero, / y sin carne en las costillas.

207

Segador, tírate afuera,
dexa entrar la espigaderuela.

Francisco Salinas, *De musica*, 1577 (text
from Alín, No. 648).

208

Estoy a la sombra
y estoy sudando.
¿Qué harán mis amores,
que andan segando?

Correas, *Vocabulario*.

Cf. a modern version from the province of Madrid: Cuando canta la chicharra, /
¡madre mía, qué calor! / Estoy a la sombra y sudo, / ¿qué será mi amante al sol?
(See Frenk Alatorre, 'Supervivencias', No. 56.)

Olive-gathering

209

La aceituna en el olivo,
si no la coges, se pasa.
Así te has de pasar tú,
si tu padre no te casa.

El Payo, Salamanca (Schindler, No. 498).

210

Apañar aceituna,
dicen que es vicio;
que poco la apañaba
la que lo dijo.

Valverde del Fresno, Cáceres (Schindler,
No. 392).

l. 1, *Apañar*, 'to pick, gather'.

211

Apañando aceitunas
se hacen las bodas,
y el que no va a aceituna
no se enamora.

Valverde del Fresno, Cáceres (Schindler,
No. 393).

l. 1, *Apañando*, 'picking, gathering'.

212
¿Qué tendrán, madre,
para cosas de amores
los olivares?

Andalucía (Molina, p. 135).

The lullaby

García Lorca saw in the Spanish lullaby a basic difference from the usual 'canción de cuna europea, suave y monótona, a la cual puede entregarse el niño con toda fruición, desplegando todas sus aptitudes para el sueño': a conflict between the mother's love and her 'desgana de la vida', an attempt to stir as well as to soothe (see *Las nanas infantiles, Obras*, pp. 91–108). While the incidence of melancholy, of ideas of deprivation and death, is quite high, this judgement is not borne out by the majority of *nanas*, many of which are full of the affection and selflessness normal in the lullaby.

213
La palomita canta
en el olivu;
cállate, palomita,
que duerma el niñu.

Montehermoso, Cáceres (Schindler, No. 362).

214
El mi chiqueninu
se quieri dormil,
y el pícaru sueñu
no quieri venil.

Montehermoso, Cáceres (Schindler, No. 362).

l. 1, *chiqueninu*, 'little one'; ll. 2, 4, *dormil* and *venil* are infinitives.
Cf. a version from Buenos Aires: Este niño lindo se quiere dormir, / y el pícaro sueño no quiere venir. / Hágale la cama en el toronjil; / y en la cabecera póngale un jazmín, / que con su fragancia me la haga dormir. (R. Menéndez Pidal, *Los Romances de América*, Buenos Aires, 1939, p. 44.)

215

Mi niño es una rosa,
mi niño es un clavel,
mi niño es un espejo,
su madre se mira en él.

San Martín de Trevejo, Cáceres
(Schindler, No. 374).

Cf. this wedding song from León: La madrina es una rosa, / el padrinu es un clavel, / la novia yía un espeju / ya el noviu se mira en él. (Álvarez, p. 108.)

216

En los brazos te tengo,
y me da espanto.
¿Qué será de ti, niño,
si yo te falto?

Andalucía (Pohren, p. 117).

217

Clavelito encarnado,
rosa en capullo,
duérmete, vida mía,
mientras te arrullo.

Andalucía (Pohren, p. 118).

218

Nana, nana, nana,
ay, nana,
duérmete, lucerito
de la mañana.

Andalucía (Pohren, p. 118).

219

Duerme el niño en la cuna,
y dice su madre:
— Calla, que viene el coco.
Y era su padre.

5   Coco, coquito,
    coco, no vengas,
    mira que no es tuyo
    ni un pelo siquiera.

Madrid (Torner, *Lírica*, No. 87).

220

A la nana, niño mío,
a la nanita y haremos
en el campo una chocita
y en ella nos meteremos.

Guadix, Granada (García Lorca, *Las
nanas infantiles*, *Obras*, p. 101).

221

Ora, ora, niño, ora;
¿quién vos hai de dar la teta
si tu pai va no monte
y tua mai na leña seca?

Orense (García Lorca, *Las nanas infantiles*,
Obras, p. 103).

l. 2, *vos hai de dar*, 'is to give you'; l. 3, *pai*, 'father'; *no*, 'in the'; l. 4, *tua mai*, 'your mother'; *na*, 'in the'.

Death

Just as the traditional love lyric, while usually adhering to its own conventions, is free from those conventions which garb and eventually strangle the medieval courtly love lyric, so the relatively few traditional poems on death appear to have been composed in ignorance of the late medieval stylizations of the death theme. The horror and universality of death are paramount elements in the court literature and graphic art of the later Middle Ages; Spanish court poetry on the subject is generally impersonal and discursive, a vehicle for turgid Christian moralizing in the *de contemptu mundi* convention, or for displays of classical erudition in the regurgitated *ubi sunt?* theme. When the traditional lyric turns to death, it does not turn away from love. It is usually concerned with the individual response to the death of the beloved. The limited format compresses and heightens the single anonymous grief, in some cases with an obsessively repetitive phrasing, so that the emotion strains the limits of the poem. Universality is attained not by the clod-hopping pointing of a moral but by our identifying with the bereaved singer into whose mind we see.

222

Mira que te mira Dios,
mira que te está mirando;
mira que te has de morir,
mira que no sabes cuando.

Hinojosa, Soria (Schindler, No. 677).

This is widely known, and is several centuries old (see Frenk Alatorre, 'Supervivencias', No. 70).

223

En Ávila, mis ojos,
dentro en Ávila.

En Ávila del Río
mataron a mi amigo,
5   dentro en Ávila.

CMP, No. 215.

224

Llorad las damas, sí Dios os vala,
Guillén Peraza quedó en la Palma
la flor marchita de la su cara.

No eres palma, eres retama,
5   eres ciprés de triste rama,
eres desdicha, desdicha mala.

Tus campos rompan tristes volcanes,
no vean placeres, sino pesares,
cubran tus flores los arenales.

10 Guillén Peraza, Guillén Peraza,
¿dó está tu escudo, dó está tu lanza?
Todo lo acaba la malandanza.

Text from *Antología*, No. 7.

l. 1, *si Dios os vala*, 'may God save you'; l. 2, *quedó*, 'left'; l. 11, *¿dó . . . ?*,
'where . . . ?'.

The editors' note reads: 'Endechas cantadas en Canarias a la muerte de Guillén
Peraza (1443). Las recogió de la tradición oral en 1632 Abreu Galindo. Seguimos el
texto en trísticos monorrimos según aparece en José Pérez Vidal, *Endechas populares
en trísticos monorrimos*, La Laguna, 1952, pág. 38.'

225

No soy yo quien ser solía,
no, no, no,
sombra soy del que murió.

*Segunda parte de la Silva de varios
romances*, 1550 (text from Alín, No. 5).

226

Quando de mi dueño
se escapa el alma,
como cierva herida
me arrojo al agua.

'Romancerillos', No. 52.

227

— Dezilde a la muerte, madre,
que no me lleve.
— Arto le digo, hija,
y ella no quiere.

Foulché-Delbosc, 'Séguedilles', No. 12.

l. 1, *Dezilde*, an old form of *Decidle*; l. 3, *Arto*, 'enough'.

228

Por el chaparralito
no quiero ya pasar,
porque se me ha muerto mi niño de mi alma,
y me echo a llorar.

R. Molina and A. Mairena, *Mundo y formas del cante flamenco*, Madrid, 1970, p. 130.

229

Reza un paternoster
por Juan Fernández.
— ¿Jesús, y muerto ié?
— No, sino que vo a matarle.

Correas, *Vocabulario*.

l. 3, *ié*, a dialect form of *es*; l. 4, *vo a*, 'I am going to'.

Local pride and rivalry

Most Spanish villages have rhymes in their own praise, and others
ridiculing neighbouring settlements. The large collection one could
make of verses similar to those contained in this section would be of
small poetic merit, and very repetitive; in many cases a verse serves
different areas, varied only by the substitution of one name for another.

230

Moraleja la llana,
corral de putas;
Santibáñez el Alto,
también hay muchas.

Cáceres.

231

Fuentecambrón en alto,
Cenegro en vega,
la villa de Valdanzo
la flor se lleva.

Soria (Schindler, p. 126).

232

Cachorilla y la Pescueza
son dos bonitos lugares,
que ellos solitos se alaban,
porque no hay quien los alabe.

Cáceres.

233

En Magallón,
en cada casa un ladrón;
y en la casa del alcalde,
el hijo y el padre.

Zaragoza (Rodríguez Marín, *Refranes*,
p. 189).

234

En Mantiel,
rascan la piel.

Guadalajara (Rodríguez Marín, *Refranes*,
p. 190).

Nostalgia and homesickness

235

Soledad tengo de ti,
tierra mía do nací.

Si muriere sin ventura
sepúltenme en alta sierra,
5 porque no extrañe la tierra
mi cuerpo en la sepultura;
y en sierra de grande altura,
por ver si veré de allí
las tierras a do nací.
10 Soledad tengo de ti,
¡oh!, tierras donde nací.

Vásquez, *Recopilación*, II, 20.

l. 2, *do*, 'where'.

236
¡Ay de mí, que en tierra agena
me veo sin alegría!
¿Cuándo me veré en la mía?

C. *Upsala*, No. XXII.

237

Pues que en esta tierra
no tengo a nadie,
aires de la mía
vení a llevarme.

5 Pues que en esta tierra
no tengo amor,
aires de la mía
lleváme al albor.

R. Menéndez Pidal, 'Cartapacios literarios
salmantinos', *Boletín de la Academia
Española*, I, 1914, p. 311.

Cf. Correas, *Arte*, p. 448: Aires de mi tierra, / vení y llevadme, / questoy en tierra
axena, / no tengo a nadie.

238
Adiós, pueblo del Guijito,
las espaldas te voy dando.
Yo no sé qué queda dentro,
que mis ojos van llorando.
5 ¡Arriba, paloma, y sube!,
que mis ojos van llorando.

Guijo de Galisteo, Cáceres.

239
Valverde de mi Valverde,
Valverde de mi consuelo,
¡quién estuviera en Valverde,
aunque durmiera en el suelo,
5 debajo de un pino verde!

Andalucía (Molina, p. 139).

240

Airiños da miña terra,
airiños do meu lugar,
airiños, airiños, aires,
aires, vindeme a buscar.

Galicia (Torner, *Lírica*, No. 3).

l. 1, *da miña terra*, 'of my country'; l. 2, *do meu lugar*, 'of my village'; l. 4, *vindeme a buscar*, 'come and find me'.

241

Llévame a la trasera
del carro, Pedro,
para así estar más cerca
del bien que dejo.

Castile (Torner, *Lírica*, No. 139).

Torner also quotes seventeenth- and eighteenth-century versions.

PART II

A series of examples, with explanatory and critical comments, showing that the traditional lyric rises in literary esteem at certain periods, that its forms and themes are adapted by writers whose production is not limited to such verse, and that its contribution to the richness of their work is great, varied and lasting, a consistent thread woven through Spanish literature and binding it to the roots of the Spanish people.

> Deja, la morenita,
> lo que no es tuyo:
> deja los estudiantes
> hir al estudio.

Foulché-Delbosc, 'Séguedilles', No. 17.

A. An Arabic *muwashshaḥa*

The oldest extant lyrics in a romance language are the fragments used
as the *kharjas* of Arabic and Hebrew *muwashshaḥas*.[4] The *muwashshaḥa*
form appears to have originated in Andalucía when the south of Spain
was occupied by the Arabs, and to have spread to other parts of the
Arab world. To compose a *muwashshaḥa* one first had to settle on a
kharja, a two-, three- or four-line ending for the poem; the rhyme-scheme
of the stanzas leading up to this ending could only be established after
the writing or selection of the *kharja*, as the latter's rhymes appeared
also in the body of the *muwashshaḥa*. A poem written in, say, North
Africa would be in Classical Arabic, with the exception of the *kharja*,
which would be in Vulgar Arabic. An Arab poet in Spain, however,
had two subordinate linguistic vehicles to choose from when deciding on
a *kharja*: Vulgar Arabic, and the romance dialect spoken by the
mozárabes, descendants of those people of the Visigothic kingdom of
Spain who remained in the areas conquered by the Arabs in the early
eighth century, and maintained their romance dialects under the rule
of the Arabs, some of whom became bilingual. As a result of this
situation, some of the Peninsular *muwashshaḥas* have as their *kharjas*
fragments of Mozarabic popular verse. This is the earliest manifestation
of a practice which is readopted in several later periods: the inclusion
in a courtly poem of a fragment of popular verse which provides its
climax, nucleus or key. There are also *muwashshaḥas* in Hebrew with
Mozarabic *kharjas*.

---

[4] Other spellings of *kharja* and *muwashshaḥa* include *jarcha, jarŷa* and *kharǧa*;
muwassaḥa and *moaxaja*. Some scholars preserve the Arabic ending of the plural:
kharjāt, muwashshaḥāt.

133

This is the normal rhyme-scheme for a *muwashshaha* with a two-line *kharja*:

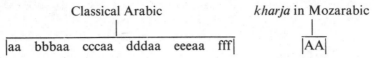

Classical Arabic   *kharja* in Mozarabic

|aa bbbaa cccaa dddaa eeeaa fff| |AA|

The *kharjas* are almost invariably love-poems, and express female emotion; several are included in Part I. If the *muwashshaha* is also a love-poem, the thematic cementing may be straightforward. Many *muwashshahas*, however, are panegyrics, so that the link with the *kharja* is more forced. In such cases the difference of theme may be overcome by a strongly erotic (often homosexual) tone in the eulogy, or by a cleverly worded final stanza giving the *kharja* some point of relevance to the rest of the poem. I give below a translation of such a *muwashshaha* preserving the Mozarabic of the three-line *kharja*. The poem is a eulogy of King al-Ma'mūn of Toledo (1037–75) by Abū Bakr Muḥammad ibn Isà. The *kharja*, as is usual, contrasts with the rest of the poem not only in its language, but also in style, tone and content.

    a   Now then, my critic, I have thrown off all restraint,
    a   and will not abstain
    a   from gazelles of human kind, or from drinking wine.

    b   What is life but the love of a gentle gazelle,
5   b   slender and dusky; and the stimulation of cups
    b   of wine like the sun's rays,
    a   as though there is in its cup when one turns it
    a   a brand of fire
    a   which the [spout of the] jug twists like the twisted bracelet?

10 c   There are two things for which my heart longs:
    c   speaking with the young, and drinking wine.
    c   Where they are concerned, I brook no censure.
    a   No, [I swear it by] the bearer of the crown of glory,
    a   who makes the rivers flow
15 a   with the floods of his munificence, and protects the home;

d King al-Ma'mūn, he of the noble attributes,

d the one, the unique, rich in good qualities.

d How many eulogies has he brought to life, how many cares done to death!

a His right hand brings rivers of gold upon us,

20 a while the left

a illumines the gloom of poverty with the full moon of wealth.

e In his name is an augury of victory and conquest.

e Benefit has spread everywhere to the people of the earth.

e He has become peerless in generosity.

25 a His noble reputation has become famous in high countries and in low,

a throughout all cities,

a so that even the camel-drivers have composed a driving-song about him.

f How many a girl complains of separation from her lover!

f and at dawn on the day of his departure, weeping

30 f on the sea-shore, she began to say:

A ¡Yā qoražōnī, ke kéreš bōn' amār!

A a liyorār

A laita[-nī 'obiese] weliyoš de mār.

l. 31, *qoražōnī*, 'heart'; *ke kéreš*, 'you who wish' (or 'want'); *bōn'*, 'good'; l. 32, *liyorār*, 'to weep'; l. 33, *laita[-nī 'obiese]*, 'would that I had'; *weliyoš*, 'eyes' (diminutive).

The transliterated Arabic text may be found in García Gómez, No. XXIX. García Gómez's version of the *kharja*, here reproduced, is rather speculative: slight tampering with the text in the *liyorār* of the thirty-second line, and a conjectural restoration of the first half of the thirty-third, produces a plausible result. The difficulties of restoring the *kharjas* are numerous: the Arabic and Hebrew scripts in which they survive reproduce only the consonantal sounds, and many of the texts have probably deteriorated through being copied by monolingual scribes to whom the *kharja* was simply a meaningless string of consonants.

It is possible that the whole of the last stanza may be intended to represent the song referred to in the penultimate stanza, i.e. that the *kharja* is a song within a song within a poem. This sounds complicated, but this situation is certainly found in the *gallego* poem of the following section.

On the *kharjas*, see Dámaso Alonso, 'Cancioncillas de amigo mozárabes', *Revista de Filología Española*, XXXIII (1949), pp. 297–349; R. Menéndez Pidal, 'Cantos románicos andalusíes. Continuadores de una lírica latina vulgar', *Boletín de la Real*

Academia Española, XXXI (1951), pp. 187–270; E. García Gómez, 'La lírica hispano-árabe y la aparición de la lírica románica', *Al-Andalus*, XXI (1956), pp. 303–38. On the problems of the restoration and interpretation of the texts, see R. Hitchcock, 'Some doubts about the Reconstruction of the *Kharjas*', *Bulletin of Hispanic Studies*, L (1973), pp. 109–19.

B. The *cancioneiro* poets' interest in the popular

Broadly speaking, the medieval court poets writing love-poetry in *gallego* have two basic stylistic uniforms. The *cantiga de amor* is masculine in viewpoint, and its theme is courtly love. The *cantiga de amigo* is feminine in viewpoint, and owes much to the non-courtly themes and forms of the native lyric of the Peninsula. These two types, however, are written in many cases by the same poets, and the dividing lines between the two are not always hard and fast. The *cantiga de amor* is largely a courtly convention, but it is difficult to decide how far the *cantiga de amigo*, certainly a convention, has been made courtly, regularized, prettified, and how closely it reproduces the character of the popular lyrics on which it is somehow based, since these were never recorded. The *cantiga de amigo* goes hand-in-hand with the *cosaute* form, but it may be that the establishment of the *cosaute* as a courtly convention led to a greater regularization of a parallelism which at the level of popular dance was employed with greater variation and fluidity (though modern field-work has revealed oral *cosautes* with just the same form as the *cancioneiro* lyrics). Certainly the *cantiga de amigo* provides the main body of evidence feeding our speculation about popular Iberian verse of the early period.

I have included a number of *cantigas de amigo* in Part I, and see no need to insert another here, but the reader should bear in mind the extreme importance of the *genre* as the principal manifestation of courtly interest in popular verse in the thirteenth and fourteenth centuries. As a different example of this interest I include below a poem by the thirteenth-century court poet Airas Nunes. This is a kind of *pastourelle* built around short pieces of popular verse. Such a mixture is a rarity in the *cancioneiros*, but provides a link of method between the *muwashshaha* and the Castilian poem of Section C: the mode of inserting the fragments, as songs in the mouth of a character in the

poem, is the same in all three, as is the attitude to the inserted material,
objective interest rather than immersion and assimilation.

> Oy oj' eu hua pastor cantar,
> d' u cavalgava per hua ribeyra,
> e a pastor estava senlheyra;
> e ascondi-me pola ascuytar,
> 5 e dizia muy bem este cantar:
> — So lo ramo verde frolido,
> vodas fazen a meu amigo;
> choran olhos d' amor.

> E a pastor parecia muy ben,
> 10 e chorava e estava cantando,
> e eu muy passo fuy-m' achegando
> pola oyr, e sol non faley rem;
> e dizia este cantar muy bem:
> — ¡Ay! estorninho do avelanedo,
> 15 cantades vos e moyr' eu e peno,
> e d' amores ey mal.

> E eu oy a sospirar enton,
> e queyxava-se estando con amores,
> e fazia guirlanda de flores;
> 20 desy chorava muy de coraçon,
> e dizia este cantar enton:
> — ¡Que coyta ey tan grande de sofrer!
> Amar amigo e non ousar veer;
> e pousarey so lo avelanal.

> 25 Poys que a guirlanda fez a pastor,
> foy-se cantando indo-s' en manselinho,
> e torney-m' eu logo a meu camyno,
> ca de a nojar non ouve sabor;
> e dizia este cantar ben a pastor:

30   — Pela ribeyra do rio,
       cantando ya la virgo
       d' amor:
       — Quem amores ha,
       ¿como dormirá?
35   ¡Ay, bela frol!

CBN, No. 811.

l. 1, *oy oj' eu,* 'I heard today'; *hua pastor,* 'a shepherdess'; l. 2, *d' u,* 'from where';
l. 3, *a,* 'the'; *senlheyra,* 'alone'; l. 4, *ascondi-me,* 'I hid'; *pola ascuytar,* 'to listen to
her'; l. 5, *bem,* 'well'; l. 6, *So lo,* 'under the'; *frolido,* 'flowering'; l. 8, *choran,* 'are
weeping'; *olhos,* 'eyes'; l. 11, *passo,* 'quietly'; *fuy-m'* *achegando,* 'drew near'; l. 12,
sol non faley rem, 'I said not a word'; l. 15, *moyr' eu,* 'I am dying'; l. 17, *E eu oy a
sospirar enton,* 'And then I heard her sigh'; l. 20, *desy chorava,* 'then she wept'; l. 22,
coyta, 'trouble'; l. 25, *Poys que,* 'after'; *a,* 'the'; *fez,* 'made'; l. 26, *indo-s' en manselinho,*
'going away slowly'; l. 27, *logo,* 'then'; l. 28, *ca,* 'for'; *a nojar,* 'to hurt her'; *non ouve
sabor,* 'I had no wish'.

C. The Marqués de Santillana's

Villancico a unas tres fijas suyas

Iñigo López de Mendoza, Marqués de Santillana (1398–1458),
exempted by wealth and position from the mercenary attitude to
literature which characterizes many of the numerous other poets of the
reign of John II, is able to read more widely and to dabble and
experiment in a more varied range of *genres* than most of his
contemporaries. While he himself would almost certainly set greater
importance on his longer, overtly Italianate *decires,* and while he writes
scornfully in his *Carta e Prohemio* of the literary tastes of the 'gente de
baja e servil condición', it is his shorter and more traditional verse that
his modern readers usually find more appealing. He is among the earliest
poets writing in Castilian to attempt to dignify the popular tradition for
the courtly audience. Some of his *serranillas,* for example, smooth the
rough edges of the Spanish *serrana* tradition and bring to it something
of the delicacy of the French *pastourelle.* The following *Villancico* is
one of the first Castilian examples of the incorporation into a courtly
poem of fragments of popular verse. The simple method of insertion,
by making the figures in the poem, in their conventional *locus amoenus,*
sing the traditional fragments, is not that adopted by most of Santillana's

successors, but is very similar to that employed earlier in *gallego* by Airas Nunes. There is still no attempt at a real blend of courtly and popular, but only a juxtaposition; except for the traditional fragments, the poem differs little in style from many of the *decires* of the period.

> Por una gentil floresta
> de lindas flores e rosas
> vide tres damas fermosas,
> que de amores han recuesta.
> 5   Yo con voluntat muy presta
> me llegué a conoscellas;
> començó la una de ellas
> esta canción tan honesta:
> — Aguardan a mí;
> 10   nunca tales guardas vi.
>
> Por mirar su fermosura
> d'estas tres gentiles damas,
> yo cobríme con las ramas,
> metíme so la verdura.
> 15   La otra con grand tristura
> començó de sospirar
> e decir este cantar
> con muy honesta messura:
> — La niña que amores ha,
> 20   sola, ¿cómo dormirá?
>
> Por no les facer turbança,
> no quise ir más adelante
> a las que con ordenança
> cantavan tan consonante.
> 25   La otra con buen semblante
> dixo: Señoras de estado,
> pues las dos avéis cantado,
> a mí conviene que cante:
> — Dejatlo al villano pene;
> 30   véngueme Dios d'elle.

Desque ya ovieron cantado
estas señoras que digo,
yo salí desconsolado
como ome sin abrigo.
35   Ellas dixeron: Amigo,
non soys vos el que buscamos;
mas cantat, pues que cantamos:
— Sospirando yva la niña,
e non por mí,
40   que yo bien se lo entendí.

Santillana, Canciones y decires, ed.
V. García de Diego, Clásicos castellanos,
Madrid, 1932, pp. 214–16.

l. 3, *vide*, 'I saw'; l. 6, *conoscellas*, an old form of *conocerlas*; l. 14, *so*, 'under';
l. 34, *ome*, 'man'.
   In one manuscript this poem is attributed to Suero de Ribera (see Alín, No. 8, note).
Santillana adopts an identical method, but inserts courtly fragments, in his *Querella
de amor* (*Canciones y decires*, pp. 136–42). Of the *Villancico* fragments, the first
should be compared with Part I, No. 35 and the second with Part I, Nos. 25, 26, 27
and 37, and with the last three lines of the Airas Nunes poem in Part II, Section B.
For Santillana's *serranillas*, see *Canciones y decires*, pp. 225–41.

D. Gil Vicente

   The traditional lyrics in the plays of Gil Vicente (1465?–1537) are
included for their intrinsic charm, for dramatic variation, and as an
element of popular rural colour. They are sung, and are not, as a rule,
integrated with the dialogue (an exception is the farcical scene in *Quem
tem farelos?*, in which Aires Rosado's serenade is interrupted by the
punning comments of his servant). In many cases, in fact, the content of
the lyric has no connection with the plot at all. It is often impossible to
tell whether Gil Vicente has plucked a whole song out of the popular
tradition, glossed an existing *estribillo*, or written refrain and gloss
himself, although in a few cases there are other versions of a song or its
refrain elsewhere, including one or two modern oral versions. If the
lyrics not found elsewhere are his own work, then his touch is perfect,
his assimilation of the tone and rhythms of popular song total. With

him the *culto/popular* distinction, clear in the work of Santillana a
century earlier, crumbles, and we have a *lírica tradicional*, of equal
contemporary appeal on either level (though in fact, in the context of the
plays, directed towards the amusement of the Portuguese court).

The greatest concentration of his lyrics is in a play written to celebrate
the birth of a daughter to João III in 1527, the *Tragicomedia pastoril da
Serra da Estrela*, from which the following extracts are taken. The mode
of introducing the lyrics is rather stylized: each new shepherd or
shepherdess enters singing; the songs could in most cases be interchanged
or replaced by others without disruption of the play.

> . . . *Vem Gonçalo, hum pastor da Serra, que vem
> da Corte, e vem cantando.*

> —Volaba la pega y vaise;
> quem me la tomasse.

> 5   Andaba la pega
> no meu cerrado,
> olhos morenos,
> bico dourado;
> quem me la tomasse.

> 10   Pardeos, mui alvoroçada
> anda a nossa Serra agora!

> *Serra* Gonçalo, venhas embora . . .

> *Obras completas*, Vol. IV, p. 194.

l. 1, *Vem*, 'enters, comes'; *da*, 'of the, from the'; *Serra*, 'Sierra'; l. 6, *no meu*, 'in
my'; l. 7, *olhos*, 'eyes'; l. 8, *bico*, 'beak'; l. 10, *Pardeos*, 'By God'; l. 11, *a nossa*, 'our';
l. 12, *venhas embora*, 'welcome'.

> . . . *Vem Fernando cantando*

> — Com que olhos me olhaste,
> que tão bem vos pareci?
> Tão asinha m'olvidaste,
> 5   quem te disse mal de mi? . . .

> *Obras completas*, Vol. IV, p. 203.

l. 2, *olhos*, 'eyes'; *me olhaste*, 'did you look at me?'; l. 3, *tão bem*, 'so well, so good';
l. 4, *Tão asinha*, 'so quickly'; l. 5, *disse*, 'spoke'.

Compare with this the following poem, quoted in Frenk Alatorre, 'Supervivencias',
No. 68, as surviving orally in Andalucía and Argentina: ¿Con qué ojitos me mirastes /
que tan bien te parecí? / ¿Y tan pronto m'orvidastes? / ¿Quién t' h' hablao mar de mí?

> . . . *Vem Madalena cantando, e Gonçalo detrás della.*
> *Cantiga*
>
> — Quando aqui chove e neva,
> que fará na serra?
>
> 5   Na serra de Coimbra
> nevava e chovia,
> que fará na serra?
>
> Gonçalo, tu a que vens?
>
> *Gonçalo*   Madalena, Madalena! . . .

Obras completas, Vol. IV, p. 207.

l. 3, *chove e neva*, 'it's raining and snowing'; l. 4, *que fará na serra?*, 'what must it
be doing in the mountains?'; l. 8, *vens*, 'come'.

In the series of songs and dances which closes the play, we are made aware of Gil
Vicente's interest in folklore and in regional variations of song and dance:

> . . . *Lopo*   Muitos ratinhos vão lá
> de ca da serra a ganhar,
> e lá os vemos cantar
> e bailar bem como ca,
> 5   e he assi desta feição.
>
> *Canta Lopo e baila, arremendando os da Serra*
>
> — E se ponerei la mano em vós,
> garrido amor.
>
> Hum amigo que eu havia
> 10   mançanas d'ouro m'envia,
> garrido amor.

Hum amigo que eu amava
mançanas d'ouro me manda,
garrido amor.

15 Mançanas d'ouro m'envia,
a melhor era partida,
garrido amor.

Isto he, ou bem ou mal,
assi como o vós fazeis . . . .

Obras completas, Vol. IV, p. 222.

l. 1, *Muitos ratinhos vão lá*, 'They often go there'; l. 2, *de ca da*, 'from this side of the'; *ganhar*, 'to graze animals'; l. 4, *ca*, 'here'; l. 5, *he*, 'it is'; *feição*, 'fashion'; l. 6, *os da*, 'the people of the'; l. 7, *se*, 'if'; *ponerei*, 'I shall put'; l. 9, *eu*, 'I'; l. 10, *ouro*, 'gold'; l. 16, *a melhor*, 'the best'; l. 19, *o*, 'it'.

Frenk Alatorre, 'Supervivencias', No. 57, notes the similarity of this to a modern Moroccan version: Un amor que yo tenía / manzanitas de oro él me vendía, / cuatro y cinco en una espiga, / la mejorcita dellas para mi amiga. / Cuatro y cinco en una rama, / la mejorcita de ellas para mi amada.

. . . Ordenaram-se todos estes pastores em chacota, como
lá se costuma, . . . e a letra he a seguinte:

— Não me firais, madre,
que eu direi a verdade.

5 Madre, hum escudeiro
da nossa Rainha
falou-me d'amores:
vereis que dizia,
eu direi a verdade.

10 Falou-me d'amores,
vereis que dizia:
quem te me tivesse
desnuda en camisa!
Eu direi a verdade.

15 *E com esta chacota se sairam, e assi se acabou.*

Obras completas, Vol. IV, pp. 223–4.

l. 1, *chacota*, a type of rural dance; l. 2, *lá se costuma*, 'is the custom there'; *he a seguinte*, 'is the following'; l. 3, *Não me firais*, 'Don't hit me'; l. 4, *eu*, 'I'; *a*, 'the'; l. 6, *da nossa Rainha*, 'of our Queen'; l. 7, *falou-me*, 'spoke to me'; l. 12, *quem te me tivesse*, 'If only I could have you'; l. 15, *se sairam*, 'exeunt'.
Compare this lyric with a very similar Castilian version in Part I, No. 34.

E. The *culto* gloss

One of the less felicitous adaptations of the traditional lyric is the *culto* gloss of the Golden Age. The basic process is no different from that normal in the traditional lyric: the anonymous *estribillo* is usually preserved, and new stanzas are written to amplify it. The differences are that the *culto* gloss is often longer, and that there is a divorce, evidently perceived and intended, between *estribillo* and gloss in respect of tone and treatment. The traditional gloss expands the *estribillo* only slightly; its syntax is uninvolved; it is able to achieve breadth by hint and symbol and allusion to the tradition of which, like its *estribillo*, it is a part. The *culto* gloss cannot let well alone; it must probe and elaborate and explain; it erects on its simple foundation the fashionable fabric of paradox and conceit, held together by syntactical filigree; the delicate *estribillo* is dissected, crushed, left lifeless. The process is an exercise of skills rather than an act of creation, and has a particular appeal for the second-rate versifier.

One of the best-known and generally most admired traditional lyrics is *De los álamos vengo, madre*, included in this book as No. 70 of Part I. With this should be compared the following *culto* gloss:

> De los álamos vengo, madre,
> de ver como los menea el aire.
>
>
> ¿Qué firmeza, madre mía,
> conmigo el amor tendrá,
> 5   si un árbol se viene y va
> adonde el viento le guía,
> si mil veces en un día
> hojas y ramas se mudan?
> Las mismas temen y dudan

10 su esperanza y mis verdades.
De los álamos vengo, madre,
de ver como los menea el aire.

Juan de Chen, *Laberinto amoroso de los
mejores romances*, 1618, ed. J. M.
Blecua, Valencia, 1953, p. 111.

As a further example of these contrasting attitudes, I give below
another pair with a common refrain. The first is from Vásquez,
Recopilación, II, 44:

Por vida de mis ojos,
el caballero,
por vida de mis ojos,
bien os quiero.

5 Por vida de mis ojos
y de mi vida,
que por vuestros amores
ando perdida.
Por vida de mis ojos,
10 el caballero,
por vida de mis ojos,
bien os quiero.

The simplicity of this is in strong contrast to the conceptual and
syntactical complication of the *culto* gloss of the same refrain:

Por vida de mis ojos,
el caballero,
por vida de mis ojos,
que bien os quiero.

5 Quier'os de manera
que fuera mejor
sufrir mi dolor
por más que muriera.
Que no lo dijera,

10   mas creed que muero
— por vida de los vuestros —
del bien qu'os quiero.

Juan Fernández de Heredia, *Obras*, ed.
F. Martí Grajales, Valencia, 1913,
pp. 163–4.

F. The gloss *a lo divino*

A feature of the late medieval and early Golden Age periods is the
glossing of a traditional love-lyric in a particular way so as to give it a
religious instead of an erotic significance. The traditional fragment used
is again the *estribillo*; this may be slightly altered, usually so as to address
the poem to God, Christ or the Virgin. Most glosses *a lo divino* do
not share the obscurity cultivated in many *culto* glosses, nor is there the
same deliberate stylistic contrast between the old *estribillo* and the new
stanzas. The nature and object of the emotion are altered, but the
simplicity and much of the charm are preserved.

In Miguel de Fuenllana's *Libro de música para vihuela, intitulado
Orphenica lyra*, Seville, 1554, fol. 137ᵛ, there is found the following
rather prosaic traditional love-lyric:

Quiero dormir y no puedo,
qu'el amor me quita el sueño.

Manda pregonar el rey
por Granada y por Sevilla
5   que todo hombre enamorado
que se case con su amiga;
qu'el amor me quita el sueño.
Quiero dormir y no puedo,
qu'el amor me quita el sueño.

10   Que se case con su amiga.
¿Qué haré, triste, cuitado,
que era casada la mía?
Qu'el amor me quita el sueño.
Quiero dormir y no puedo,
15   qu'el amor me quita el sueño.

The refrain of the above poem reappears, about fifteen years later, in the *Cancionero sevillano* (fol. 150), where it is put into the mouth of the Infant Christ and amplified by a gloss *a lo divino*:

> Quiero dormir y no puedo,
> que el amor me quita el sueño.

> ¿Cómo tengo de dormir,
> sabiendo que he de morir
> 5   por los hombres redemir
> y tornarlos a su dueño?
> El amor grande, crecido,
> a ser hombre me ha traído;
> no me consiente adormido,
> 10   aunque soy niño y pequeño.
> Quiero dormir y no puedo,
> que el amor me quita el sueño.

Santa Teresa de Ávila (1515–82), in one of the most famous glosses of this kind, maintains the basic simplicity of her traditional original (see Part I, No. 5), but addresses herself to Christ:

> Véante mis ojos,
> dulce Jesús bueno;
> véante mis ojos,
> muérame yo luego.

> 5   Vea quien quisiere
> rosas y jazmines,
> que si yo te viere
> veré mil jardines.
> Flor de serafines,
> 10   Jesús Nazareno,
> véante mis ojos,
> muérame yo luego.

No quiero contento
mi Jesús ausente,
15   que todo es tormento
a quien esto siente;
sólo me sustente
tu amor y deseo.
Véante mis ojos,
20   dulce Jesús bueno;
véante mis ojos,
muérame yo luego.

Obras, Biblioteca de Autores Españoles,
Vol. LIII, Madrid, 1930, p. 510.

On the gloss *a lo divino*, see B. W. Wardropper, *Historia de la poesía lírica a lo divino en la cristiandad occidental*, Madrid, 1958, especially pp. 151–203.

G. Juan de Timoneda's *Tres serranas*

The Golden Age cult of the pastoral, largely classical in inspiration, overlaps only slightly with the interest in popular verse. The pastoral convention produces shepherds and shepherdesses of refined sensibility, languishing in a green, alien landscape where flocks guard themselves and the north wind never blows, racked by emotions for which the cultured literary public would have thought a flesh-and-blood peasant unfitted. The idealizing of the rural also gives rise to the courtier in peasant's dress, finding brief diversion in a pasteurized and self-conscious pastoral charade. For Cervantes, whose Don Quijote meets a group of such dilettantes, such posturing is slightly ludicrous tomfoolery; for Juan de Timoneda, in the poem below, it becomes a charming game, a test of his ability in encrusting, embroidering and bejewelling the peasant garments and artefacts of his three *serranas*. As in the eggs of Fabergé, the glorious richness of the decoration is enhanced by the basic simplicity of the object decorated. There is no real pretence of aspiration to rusticity. The poet realizes the division between the two worlds, and the shallowness of the current conventions approximating them; the beauty and glitter brought to clothing and objects by their nature utilitarian serves only to accentuate the incompatibility of *corte* and *aldea.* Timoneda is not ridiculing the game, which he clearly enjoys, but he retains the awareness that it *is* a game, and not to be taken as seriously as some of his contemporaries perhaps take it.

> Tres serranas he encontrado
> al pie de una gran montaña,
> que, según su gesto y maña,
> no deben guardar ganado.
>
> 5 De seda traían y bellos
> los velos y gorguerinas,
> cordones de perlas finas
> apretando sus cabellos,
> rubios eran todos ellos,
> 10 y de seda las servillas,
> de escarlata las basquillas,
> los monjiles de brocudo.
>
> De laurel muy adornadas
> traían sus tres guirnaldas,
> 15 con diamantes y esmeraldas,
> en ejorcas y arracadas;
> antiparas plateadas,
> de carmesín los zurrones,
> de marfil con sus cachones
> 20 cada una su cayado.
>
> Ruecas de oro en su cintura
> traían y prendederos,
> de aljófar los rocaderos,
> los husos de plata pura,
> 25 seda hilando con mesura;
> y cantando esta canción;
> — ¿Dónde está mi corazón?
> por un valle se han entrado.

Text from A. Terry, *An Anthology of Spanish Poetry 1500–1700*, Pergamon, Oxford, 1965, Part I, p. 76.

l. 6, *gorguerinas*, 'ruffs'; l. 10, *servillas*, 'slippers'; l. 11, *basquillas*, 'skirts'; l. 12, *monjiles*, 'sleeves'; l. 16, *ejorcas*, 'bracelets'; *arracadas*, 'ear-rings'; l. 17, *antiparas*, 'leggings, gaiters'.

Little is known of Timoneda's life; he died in 1583. This poem is based on Santillana's *Cantar . . . a sus fijas loando la su fermosura* (*Canciones y decires*, pp. 217–20), but owes little to it except the basic concept and some of the wording of the first eight lines.

H. Lope de Vega's interweaving of drama and lyric

A high proportion of Spanish Golden Age plays are about peasants. The *costumbrismo* involved in such works includes conventional rusticisms of vocabulary, naïvety of conversation, and traditional songs and dances. In some plays the songs (*letras*) are intended to colour and enhance the unsophisticated rural background, against which the machinations of a disturber of pastoral peace, often a nobleman, are thrown into relief; the lyric is seen as symbolizing the harmony and joy of an idealized rural life. The interpolated song may also have a more functional role as a device for varying the pace of a play. It is often impossible to tell whether such songs have been written by the author of the play, or merely lifted out of the substratum of traditional oral material.

One of Lope de Vega's most developed yet unobtrusive skills is the handling of such inserted songs. It is rare for Lope's *letras* to be merely ornamental. In some cases the song is an important cog in the play's machinery: information may be conveyed by it, or it may contribute greatly to the accumulation of atmosphere or to the state of mind of a character. In the case of *El caballero de Olmedo* the play is built around an old legend whose main road of transmission to Lope was the song:

> Que de noche le mataron
> al caballero,
> la gala de Medina,
> la flor de Olmedo.

This song is itself an important feature in the action of the play: the hero overhears it sung, with a new gloss linking it closely with an earlier incident, as a prophecy of his own doom (Act 3, Scene XII).

In other plays, the *letra*, while not so important as a dramatic cog, is nevertheless carefully chosen, adapted or created so as to fit in with and reinforce the theme. In certain cases one can perceive Lope's work of adaptation of an old lyric to make it more relevant. A good case of his technique is *Peribáñez y el Comendador de Ocaña*. In addition to a *romance* conveying information which, overheard by the hero, contributes considerably to his state of mind and to the progress of the plot (Act 2, Scene XXI), the play includes three songs which, while not actually helping the action forward, are closely linked by their content with the theme of the play.

Peribáñez is about, among other things, fidelity and infidelity, trust and jealousy, purity and impurity, content and unease. The play begins with the wedding of Peribáñez and Casilda. All is harmony. Harmony is natural. The harmony of the peasant lovers is part of a wider harmony; the perfection of their union is part of Nature's perfection; Nature welcomes this proof of the basic goodness and continuity of life. All this is stressed by a song accompanying a wedding-dance in Act 1, Scene I (very probably composed by Lope):

> Dente parabienes
> el mayo garrido,
> los alegres campos,
> las fuentes y ríos.
>
> 5 Alcen las cabezas
> los verdes alisos,
> y con frutos nuevos
> almendros floridos.
>
> Echen las mañanas,
> 10 después del rocío,
> en espadas verdes
> guarnición de lirios.
>
> Suban los ganados
> por el monte mismo
> 15 que cubrió la nieve,
> a pacer tomillos.

> Y a los nuevos desposados
> eche Dios su bendición;
> parabién les den los prados,
> 20   pues hoy para en uno son. . . .

The marriage, then, like the rhythmically recurring processes of the
countryside, is natural, part of an overall harmony. The spell of the song
is broken by a tumult aroused by the arrival of the *novillo*, the young
bull which is to be fought as part of the wedding celebrations. The
Comendador is injured during the running of the bull; he then falls in
love with Casilda.

For much of the play Peribáñez is on a rack of uncertainty about the
relationship between Casilda and the Comendador; little pin-pricks of
doubt deflate his initial marital euphoria, in the face of the Comendador's
ill-concealed attempts at seduction. In Act 2, Scene VIII, the seduction
plot is taking shape: Peribáñez is absent on village business, Luján, the
Comendador's lackey, is disguised as a harvester as part of a plan to
introduce his master into Peribáñez's house, night is falling with the threat
of moral blackness to come; at this point Lope chooses to introduce
another *letra*:

> Trébole, ¡ay Jesús, cómo huele!
> Trébole, ¡ay Jesús, qué olor!
>
> Trébole de la casada,
> que a su esposo quiere bien;
> 5   de la doncella también,
> entre paredes guardada,
> que, fácilmente engañada,
> sigue su primero amor.
> Trébole, ¡ay Jesús, cómo huele!
> 10   Trébole, ¡ay Jesús, qué olor!
>
> Trébole de la soltera,
> que tantos amores muda;
> trébole de la viuda
> que otra vez casarse espera;
> 15   tocas blancas por defuera,

y el faldellín de color.
Trébole, ¡ay Jesús, cómo huele!
Trébole, ¡ay Jesús, qué olor!

The *estribillo* of this song is old, and is glossed elsewhere anonymously
and by other Golden Age writers (see Part I, No. 83; Torner, *Lírica*,
No. 1, gives eight other examples). The *trébole* occurs commonly in other
lyrics, being associated with the feast of St. John, and with the finding
of a lover for which the feast is traditionally a setting (see Part I, No. 199).
Lope takes this old chorus and, in the familiar manner, writes a new
gloss for it; the wording of this is not merely casual, but echoes and
reinforces the content of the song's new setting, the play. Without any
strain or unreality, and preserving the combination of statement and
symbolism characteristic of the traditional lyric, Lope introduces into
the song the ideas of fidelity and infidelity, true love and careless love.
Peace has been replaced by conflict, in the relationships of the characters
and in Peribáñez's mind; the pure harmony of the earlier song is replaced
by the deceitful purity of the 'tocas blancas por defuera' through
which there peeps, with a swing of the skirt, the 'faldellín de color',
evoking ideas of warmth and desire and barely concealed sensuality.
   In Act 3, Scene XII, the Comendador's musicians sing to Casilda a
song recalling the incident of the bull in Act 1:

> Cogióme a tu puerta el toro,
> linda casada;
> no dijiste: Dios te valga.
>
> El novillo de tu boda
> 5   a tu puerta me cogió;
> de la vuelta que me dió
> se rió la villa toda;
> y tú, grave y burladora,
> linda casada,
> 10   no dijiste: Dios te valga.

This song was almost certainly written by Lope especially for the play,
but he is careful not to make this too obvious. Stylistically, the song

reproduces perfectly the lightness and succinctness of his traditional models; the beautifully expressive concision of 'grave y burladora', the understatement of 'no dijiste: Dios te valga', reveal Lope's love for the outwardly simple but brilliantly expressive stylistic resources of the old lyric. The song does not describe exactly the earlier incident: the Comendador was not *cogido* by the bull, but fell when his horse stumbled. The wording recalls to us the beginning of the chain of events which the Comendador now hopes is near culmination, but the sophistication of Lope's technique makes it just slightly oblique, where a lesser writer might have used a more direct allusion to smaller effect. The bull has associations of lust, strength and desire; the phallic horn; the horns of cuckoldry. Elsewhere in the play (Act 3, Scene XXVII) Peribáñez compares himself to a bull, and describes the Comendador's deceiving gifts to him as 'las armas / que al toro pudieran servir de capa'. Thus the 'Cogióme a tu puerta el toro' lyric is prophetic as well as retrospective: the Comendador is to be killed at Casilda's door by Peribáñez, the man on whose head he has tried to set the cuckold's horns, the bull he has tried to confuse as he tried to bemuse the *novillo* of Act 1.

Peribáñez y el Comendador de Ocaña is in the *Biblioteca de Autores Españoles*, Vol. XLI, pp. 281–302, and in *Obras*, Vol. X, pp. 107–47. The imagery of the bull in the play is the subject of a study by E. M. Wilson, 'Images et structure dans "Peribáñez" ', *Bulletin Hispanique*, LI (1949), pp. 125–59. The many other Golden Age plays containing interesting lyric insertions include Lope's *El caballero de Olmedo* (*Obras*, Vol. X, pp. 149–85), *El villano en su rincón* (*Obras*, Vol. XV, pp. 273–312), *La serrana de la Vera* (*Obras*, Vol. XII, pp. 1–43), *El cardenal de Belén* (*Obras*, Vol. IV, pp. 151–86) and *La venta de la zarzuela* (*Obras*, Vol. III, pp. 47–62), and Tirso de Molina's *La mejor espigadera*, *La venganza de Tamar* and *Antona García* (*Comedias*, ed. Cotarelo y Mori, E., Vol. I, *Nueva Biblioteca de Autores Españoles*, Vol. IV, pp. 311–42, 407–33, 616–44). See also Wilson, E. M. and Sage, J., *Poesías líricas en las obras dramáticas de Calderón*, London, 1964.

I. A Góngora *letrilla*

The first two lines of the following poem by Luis de Góngora (1561–1627) could, by their content and style, be popular, but from line 3 onwards we are on a new literary level. The goosegirl and her charges are frozen in a frame, bright under a new, probing, penetrating light. Allusion is not to concepts and images traditional in the lyric, but to classical myth; syntax is complex; metaphor is chosen to make us doubt

our previous awareness of the world, to dissolve and reassemble our
sensual impressions. We see Nature through the lens of Art; this does
not distort, but rather clarifies, making outlines and sensual limits hard
and exact, replacing plasticity with rigidity, the warm and the fluid with
the icy and the solid, mutability and confusion with permanence and
precision. There is no narrative, no human contact, no emotion. As in
Timoneda's *serrana* poem, the effect stems largely from the contrast
between the acknowledged traditionalism and simplicity of the form and
basic content and the novelty, complication and richness of Góngora's
language and imagery.

> Ánsares de Menga
> al arroyo van:
> ellos visten nieve,
> él corre cristal.
>
> 5 El arroyo espera
> las hermosas aves,
> que cisnes suaves
> son de su ribera;
> cuya Venus era
> 10 hija de Pascual.
> Ellos visten nieve,
> él corre cristal.
>
> Pudiera la pluma
> del menos bizarro
> 15 conducir el carro
> de la que fué espuma;
> en beldad, no en suma,
> lucido caudal.
> Ellos visten nieve,
> 20 él corre cristal.
>
> Trenzado el cabello
> le sigue Minguilla,
> en la verde orilla

           desnudo el pie bello;
25   granjeando en ello
           marfil oriental.
           Ellos visten nieve,
           él corre cristal.

           La agua apenas trata
30   cuando dirás que
           se desata el pie,
           y no se desata;
           plata dando a plata
           con que, liberal,
35   ellos visten nieve,
           él corre cristal.

> Luis de Góngora, *Romances y letrillas*,
> ed. P. Henríquez Ureña, Buenos Aires,
> 1939, p. 259.

J. The nineteenth century; a renewed interest in folklore. A *cantar gallego* by Rosalía de Castro

During about a century and a half after its Golden Age vogue, the
traditional lyric is neglected by reputable poets and dramatists and their
literate public, and the continuance of the tradition at the popular level
is, in consequence, largely undocumented. Early nineteenth-century
ideas on the purity and inherent superiority of popular poetry made less
impact on contemporary Spanish literature than on that of the German
Romantics, but there is a certain revival of interest in folklore in Spain
which produces a climate in which interaction can again occur. Among
scholarly works manifesting and stimulating this interest are editions
and studies of the *romancero* by Agustín Durán (1793–1862). The novels
of Fernán Caballero (the pseudonym of Cecilia Böhl de Faber (1796–1877))
are depictions of popular Andalusian life in which local colour, familiar
conversation and rural pastimes are important; the same author was in
the vanguard of the modern collecting movement, and left a collection
of Andalusian proverbs and songs. Among mid-century poets influenced

by and closely imitating popular lyrics are the second-rank figures
Antonio de Trueba (1819–89), who, inspired by the traditional forms
of the Basque Country, wrote poems and songs, composed ' ¿cómo sé?,
a la buena de Dios, como el pueblo compone los suyos', and Augusto
Ferrán (1836–80), whose volumes of *cantares*, *La Soledad* (1861) and
La Pereza (1871), are a further attempt to restore to contemporary
poetry the directness and vitality of the popular lyric.

The renewed reverence for the popular lyric as a *Naturpoesie* in the
mid-nineteenth century is evident in Francisco Giner de los Ríos' article
'Poesía erudita y poesía vulgar' (1863): '. . . la poesía popular, riquísima
elaboración del sentimiento de un pueblo . . . , eco armonioso de su
vida interior, . . . es, en efecto, la más alta manifestación que hacen de
sí las naciones, y la comprobación más enérgica de su existencia propia;
en ella, el poeta es la patria . . .'.

Gustavo Adolfo Bécquer's more percipient interest in the popular is
most explicitly expressed in his prologue to his friend Ferrán's *La
Soledad*. His praise of the popular lyric is inspired by its brevity, vitality
and allusiveness: 'Hay otra [poesía] natural, breve, seca, que brota del
alma como una chispa eléctrica, que hiere el sentimiento con una palabra
y huye, y desnuda de artificio, desembarazada dentro de una forma libre,
despierta, con una que las toca, las mil ideas que duermen . . .; en cuyas
producciones se vierte el genio de los pueblos más espontáneamente con
el genio mismo del poeta, quien sólo atiende a contener en la expresión
anterior los pensamientos y emociones que halla en su alma, y que
desbordan con su entusiasta calor y lozanía el cauce de la palabra,
estrecho e incompleto para la inmensidad de su riqueza.'

Bécquer's prologue praises Ferrán's *cantares* for capturing and
refining these characteristics, but his own poetry is in fact, in what it
leaves unsaid, a much more subtle and successful example of their
influence. I regret that considerations of space make it impossible to
include examples here. If this anthology were longer, then a selection of
Bécquer's *Rimas* would have high priority for inclusion.

The *Cantares gallegos* (1863) of Rosalía de Castro (1837–85) were
written in a period when field-workers were only beginning systematically
to collect surviving oral material. They are inspired by the author's
first-hand acquaintance, from childhood onwards, with the folk-songs
of Galicia, as she is at pains to explain in her prologue: '. . . n'abendo

deprendido en máis escola qu'á d'os nosos probes aldeans, guiada sólo
por aqueles cantares, aquelas palabras cariñosas e aqueles xirons nunca
olvidados que tan doçemente resoaron nos meus oídos desd'á cuna, e
que foran recollidos pó-lo meu coraçón como harencia propia, atrevínme
a escribir estos cantares, esforzándome en dar a conocer cómo algunhas
d'as nosas poéticas costumes inda conservan certa frescura patriarcal
e primitiva, e cóm' ó noso dialecto doçe e sonoro é tan a propósito com'
ó pirmeiro prá toda clase de versificación.'

Rosalía's prologue burns with a defensive pride in the beauty,
language and character of her Galician homeland; the *Cantares* are
pervaded by *morriña*, the homesickness of the *gallego*, accentuated by
Rosalía's loathing of the bright barrenness of Castile, where she was
forced to live by her husband's employment. The popular fragment at
the beginning of the following poem should be compared with Nos. 237
and 240 of Part I. Rosalía's highly subjective gloss, written apparently
in ignorance and certainly in neglect of Golden Age methods, picks up
words and lines of the popular song and repeats them, sometimes varied,
but there is no systematic refrain. The metre and assonance conform to
those of the song, whose repeated diminutive is also echoed here and
there in the gloss.

> Airiños, airiños aires,
> airiños da miña terra;
> airiños, airiños aires,
> airiños, levaime a ela.
>
> 5 Sin ela vivir non podo,
> non podo vivir contenta,
> qu'a donde queira que vaya,
> cróbeme unha sombra espesa.
> Cróbeme unha espesa nube
> 10 tal preñada de tormentas,
> tal de soidás preñada,
> qu' a miña vida envenena.
> Levaime, levaime, airiños,
> com' unha folliña seca,
> 15 que seca tamén me puxo

á callentura que queima.
¡Ay!, si non me levas pronto,
airiños da miña terra;
si non me levas, airiños,
20 quisáis xa non me conesan.
Qu' á frebe que de min come,
vaime consumindo lenta,
e no meu coraçonciño
tamén traidora se ceiba.

25 Fun n' outro tempo encarnada
com' á color da sireixa,
son oxe descolorida
com' os cirios d' as igrexas,
cal si unha meiga chuchona
30 a miña sangre bebera.
Voume quedando muchiña
com' unha rosa qu' inverna;
voume sin forzas quedando,
voume quedando morena,
35 cal unha mouriña moura,
filla de moura ralea.

Levaime, levaime, airiños,
levaime a donde m' esperan
unha nay que por min chora,
40 un pay que sin min n' alenta,
un hirmán por quen daría
á sangre d' as miñas venas,
e un amoriño á quen alma
e vida lle prometera.
45 Si pronto non me levades,
¡ay!, morrerei de tristeza,
soya n' unha terra extraña,
dond' extraña m' alomean,
donde todo canto miro
50 todo me dic' ¡extranxeira!

¡Ay miña pobre casiña!
¡Ay miña vaca bermella!
Años, que valás nos montes;
pombas, qu' arrulás nas eiras;
55   mozos, qu' atruxás bailando,
redobre d'as castañetas,
xás-co-rras-chás d' as cunchiñas,
xurre-xurre d' as pandeiras,
tambor do tamborileiro,
60   gaitiña, gaita gallega,
xa non m' alegras dicindo:
¡Müiñeira!, ¡müiñeira!
¡Ay!, quén fora paxariño
de leves alas lixeiras!
65   ¡Ay, con qué prisa voara
toliña de tan contenta,
para cantar á alborada
nos campos da miña terra!
Agora mesmo partira,
70   partira com' unha frecha,
sin medo as sombras da noite,
sin medo da noite negra.
E que chovera ou ventara,
e que ventara ou chovera,
75   voaría, e voaría
hastra qu' alcansase a vela.
Pero non son paxariño
e irey morrendo de pena,
xa en lágrimas convertida,
80   xa en suspiriños desfeita.

Doçe galleguiños aires,
quitadoriños de penas,
encantadores d' as auguas,
amantes d' as arboredas,
85   música d'as verdes canas
do millo d' as nosas veigas,

alegres compañeiriños,
run-run de tódalas festas,
levaime nas vosas alas
90 com' unha folliña seca.
Non permitás qu' aquí morra,
airiños da miña terra,
qu' ainda penso, que de morta
ei de sospirar por ela.
95 Ainda penso, airiños aires,
que dimpois que morta sea,
e aló pó-lo camposanto,
dond' enterrada me teñan,
pasés na calada noite
100 runxindo antr' á folla seca,
ou murmuxando medrosos
antr' as brancas calaveras,
inda dimpois de mortiña,
airiños da miña terra,
105 éivos de berrar: ¡Airiños,
airiños, levaime a ela!

l. 2, *da miña*, 'of my'; l. 4, *levaime*, 'carry me off'; l. 5, *non podo*, 'I cannot'; l. 8, *cróbeme*, 'covers me'; l. 10, *tal*, 'so'; l. 11, *soidás*, 'loneliness'; l. 14, *folliña*, 'little leaf'; l. 15, *tamén*, 'too'; *me puxo*, 'I grow twisted'; l. 16, *á*, 'in the'; l. 20, *quisáis xa non me conesan*, 'perhaps they will no longer recognize me'; l. 21, *frebe*, 'fever'; *min*, 'me'; l. 23, *no meu*, 'in my'; l. 25, *Fun*, 'I was'; l. 26, *da sireixa*, 'of the cherry'; l. 27, *son oxe*, 'today I am'; l. 28, *igrexas*, 'churches'; l. 29, *cal si*, 'as if'; *meiga*, 'witch'; *chuchona*, 'sucking'; l. 31, *muchiña*, 'shrunken, withered' (?); l. 35, *cal*, 'like'; l. 36, *filla*, 'daughter'; l. 39, *nay*, 'mother'; *chora*, 'weeps'; l. 40, *pay*, 'father'; l. 41, *hirmán*, 'brother'; l. 47, *soya*, 'alone, lonely'; l. 48, *m' alomean*, 'they show me up, point me out'; l. 49, *todo canto miro*, 'everything I look at'; l. 52, *bermella*, 'red'; l. 53, *Años*, 'little lambs'; *valás*, 'bleat'; l. 54, *pombas*, 'pigeons'; l. 55, *atruxás*, 'shout with joy'; l. 57, *cunchiñas*, 'little shells'; l. 63, *quén fora*, 'if only I were'; l. 65, *voara*, 'I would fly'; l. 66, *toliña*, 'mad'; l. 70, *frecha*, 'arrow'; l. 71, *medo*, 'fear'; *noite*, 'night'; l. 73, *que chovera*, 'let it rain'; l. 76, *a vela*, 'to see it'; l. 80, *desfeita*, 'destroyed'; l. 81, *Doçe*, 'Sweet'; l. 85, *canas*, 'canes, stalks'; l. 86, *millo*, 'maize'; l. 91, *morra*, 'I die' (subjunctive); l. 93, *ainda*, 'still, even'; l. 96, *dimpois que*, 'after'; l. 97, *aló*, 'there'; *pó-lo*, 'through the'; l. 99, *calada*, 'silent'; l. 100, *runxindo antr' á folla seca*, 'rustling among the dry leaves'; l. 102, *brancas*, 'white'; l. 103, *inda*, 'still, even'; *dimpois de mortiña*, 'after I am dead'.

The *Cantares gallegos*, with their prologue, form pp. 259–393 of Rosalía's *Obras completas*, ed. V. García Martí, Madrid, 1958. There is a bibliography for Durán in the *Historia general de las literaturas hispánicas*, Vol. IV, Part 2, Barcelona, 1957,

p. 145, and for Fernán Caballero in the *Obras completas*, ed. J. M. Castro y Calvo, Madrid (*Biblioteca de Autores Españoles*), Vol. 1, 1961, pp. clxxxiii–clxxxvii. The article by Giner de los Ríos may be found in his *Obras completas*, Madrid, 1919. For Trueba, see the selection of *Cuentos y cantares*, ed. P. A. M. Escudero, Madrid, 1959; for Ferrán, see the *Obras completas*, ed. J. P. Díaz, Madrid (*Clásicos Castellanos*), 1969 (Bécquer's prologue to *La Soledad* is on pp. 7–17); for Bécquer, see his *Rimas*, ed. J. P. Díaz, Madrid (*Clásicos Castellanos*), 1963.

K. The twentieth century. Antonio and Manuel Machado. The early lyrics of García Lorca and Alberti. The lullaby from *Bodas de sangre*

Antonio Machado (1875–1939) was the son of a prominent folklorist, and his verse was probably influenced by an awareness of his father's collections and possibly of those of other investigators such as Rodríguez Marín. His use of refrain, repetition and parallelism, while often echoing traditional technique, is unsystematized and informal. His interest in the traditional lyric, however, is evinced by his repeated references to children's singing games, by his individual and subjective treatment of such motifs as the orange and lemon, running water, the thorn, the wind, etc., and also perhaps by such minor features as his use of exclamation and dialogue, and of traditional modes of beginning a poem (*¡Ay de . . . ; ¡Y . . .* ; etc.). He is fond of using the traditional four-line *copla* for the distillation of pithy, antithetical *proverbios* such as:

> Todo pasa y todo queda;
> pero lo nuestro es pasar,
> pasar haciendo caminos,
> caminos sobre la mar.

> From *Proverbios y cantares* (*Obras*,
> Losada, Buenos Aires, 1964, p. 207).

One also finds echoes of the *copla*'s conceptual parallelism:

> Anoche soñé que oía
> a Dios, gritándome: ¡Alerta!
> Luego era Dios quien dormía,
> y yo gritaba: ¡Despierta!

> From *Proverbios y cantares* (*Obras*, p. 207);
> cf. *Adiós, vida de mi vida*, p. 29.

of other traditional structural patterns:

Los olivos grises,
los caminos blancos.
El sol ha sorbido
la color del campo . . .

From *Apuntes* (*Obras*, p. 237); cf. Part I,
No. 147.

Los ojos por que suspiras,
sábelo bien,
los ojos en que te miras
son ojos porque te ven.

From *Proverbios y cantares* (*Obras*, p. 259);
cf. *Que si soy morena*, p. 34.

and of traditional content and wording:

Desde Sevilla a Sanlúcar,
desde Sanlúcar al mar,
en una barca de plata
con los remos de coral,
5   donde vayas, marinero,
contigo me has de llevar.

From *Coplas populares y no populares
andaluzas* (*Obras*, p. 757); cf. Part I,
Nos. 111, 112 and 117.

Mientras danzáis en corro,
niñas, cantad:
Ya están los prados verdes,
ya vino abril galán.

5   A la orilla del río,
por el negro encinar,
sus abarcas de plata
hemos visto brillar.

Ya están los prados verdes,
10   ya vino abril galán.

From *Canciones* (*Obras*, p. 250); cf.
Part I, Nos. 190, 192 and 193.

Machado's brother Manuel (1874–1947) made a more deliberate and folkloric use of the traditional lyric, especially that of Andalucía, in specific popular forms:

Malagueñas, soleares
y *seguiriyas* gitanas . . .

Es el saber popular,
que encierra todo el saber:
5   que es saber sufrir, amar,
morirse y aborrecer.

Es el saber popular,
que encierra todo el saber.

From *Cante hondo* (text from M. Machado,
Antología, Buenos Aires, 1940, p. 15).

Of the poets whose early writing, in the nineteen-twenties, coincides with a further resurgence of scholarly interest in traditional verse, and particularly in the oral tradition, Rafael Alberti and Federico García Lorca are the two of whom one could best say, as Alberti himself said, that 'el manadero de lo popular les sigue mojando de agua clara su obra' (*La poesía popular en la lírica española contemporánea*, Jena–Leipzig, 1933, pp. 15–16). Alberti, alone among modern poets, in my view, deserves to be ranked with Gil Vicente and Lope for his ability to feel and reproduce the elusive qualities of the traditions by which he is inspired. This is not to say that personal elements are absent: the early collections of Alberti's verse (*Marinero en tierra* (1924), *La amante* (1925), *El alba del alhelí* (1925–6)) are strong personal statements, made largely through and within the conventions of form and content of the traditional lyric, and sometimes in direct and explicit imitation of individual anonymous poems.

García Lorca, in personalizing his lyrics, sometimes deprives them of the character of his traditional models; some of the poems in his *Poema del cante jondo* (1921), *Primeras canciones* (1922) and *Canciones* (1921–4), beautiful and delicate in themselves, seem brittle and contrived, and lacking the life which Alberti somehow retains. Whatever one's personal conclusions about their relative success, the early lyrics of Lorca and Alberti represent the latest and probably the last great literary cultivation and imitation of the traditional lyric.

Alberti

MI CORZA

En Ávila, mis ojos . . . , Siglo XV.

Mi corza, buen amigo,
mi corza blanca.

Los lobos la mataron
al pie del agua.

5   Los lobos, buen amigo,
que huyeron por el río.

Los lobos la mataron
dentro del agua.

> From *Marinero en tierra* (*Poesías completas*, Buenos Aires, 1961, p. 40). Cf. Part I, No. 223.

NANA DEL NIÑO MUERTO

Barquero yo de este barco,
sí, barquero yo.

Aunque no tenga dinero,
sí, barquero yo.

5   Rema, niño, mi remero.
No te canses, no.

Mira ya el puerto lunero,
mira, miraló.

From *Marinero en tierra* (*Poesías
completas*, pp. 41–42).

TRENES

Tren del día, detenido
frente al cardo de la vía.

— Cantinera, niña mía,
se me queda el corazón
5   en tu vaso de agua fría.

Tren de noche, detenido
frente al sable azul del río.

— Pescador, barquero mío,
se me queda el corazón
10   en tu barco negro y frío.

From *Marinero en tierra* (*Poesías completas*,
pp. 44–45).

DE GUMIEL DE HIZAN
A GUMIEL DEL MERCADO

Debajo del chopo, amante,
debajo del chopo, no.

Al pie del álamo, sí,
del álamo blanco y verde.

5   Hoja blanca tú,
hoja verde yo.

From *La amante* (*Poesías completas*,
p. 53).

García Lorca[5]

LA LOLA

Bajo el naranjo lava
pañales de algodón.
Tiene verdes los ojos
y violeta la voz.

5   ¡Ay, amor,
bajo el naranjo en flor!

El agua de la acequia
iba llena de sol,
en el olivarito
10 cantaba un gorrión.

¡Ay, amor,
bajo el naranjo en flor!

Luego, cuando la Lola
gaste todo el jabón
15 vendrán los torerillos.

¡Ay, amor,
bajo el naranjo en flor!

From *Poema del cante jondo* (*Obras*,
pp. 317–18).

REMANSILLO

Me miré en tus ojos
pensando en tu alma.

Adelfa blanca.

Me miré en tus ojos
5 pensando en tu boca.

Adelfa roja.

Me miré en tus ojos.
¡Pero estabas muerta!

Adelfa negra.

From *Primeras canciones* (*Obras*, pp.
345–6).

CANCIÓN CHINA EN EUROPA

La señorita
del abanico,
va por el puente
del fresco río.

5   Los caballeros
con sus levitas,
miran el puente
sin barandillas.

La señorita
10   del abanico
y los volantes,
busca marido.

Los caballeros
están casados,
15   con altas rubias
de idioma blanco.

Los grillos cantan
por el Oeste.

(La señorita,
20   va por lo verde.)

Los grillos cantan
bajo las flores.

(Los caballeros,
van por el Norte.)

From *Canciones* (*Obras*, pp. 370–1).

CANCIONCILLA SEVILLANA

Amanecía
en el naranjel.
Abejitas de oro
buscaban la miel.

5 ¿Dónde estará
la miel?

  Está en la flor azul,
Isabel.
En la flor,
10 del romero aquel.

  (Sillita de oro
para el moro.
Silla de oropel
para su mujer.)

15 Amanecía
en el naranjel.

From *Canciones* (*Obras*, pp. 371–2).

Both Lorca and Alberti wrote plays in which they attempted to integrate lyric material. In the case of Lorca this process is especially felicitous, and lyric and drama are interwoven more intimately and completely than in the work of any of his contemporaries or Golden Age predecessors. Alberti's play *El trébol florido* (*Teatro*, 3rd edition, Buenos Aires, 1959, Vol. I, pp. 51–112) is built around a number of traditional and traditional-type lyrics, including the same *trébole* refrain used by Lope in *Peribáñez*, but the union is unimpressive. The method of integration is hardly an advance on Lope's technique: there is a fairly rigid division between inserted lyric and normal dialogue, and although the lyrics are thematically relevant to the plot, one has the feeling that they themselves are the important thing, the play merely a framework for their preservation and presentation. We see them in a livelier context than in, say, the anthologies of Torner and Schindler, but there is a rootless feeling to them which is reinforced by the play's setting, a *Tempest*-like dream island.

In Lorca's plays lyric material is incorporated with much more variety and with much greater success. The lyric may be simply sung, in some cases by a background character, like a Lope *letra*, although, as in Lope, the content is very pertinent to the play. Often, however, the lyric is integrated into the dialogue, which takes on lyric qualities so that the frontier between dialogue and lyric becomes blurred. One of the best instances of this is the lullaby scene in *Bodas de sangre* (1933). The *Suegra* and the *Mujer* of this scene (Act 1, Scene II) are respectively mother-in-law and wife of Leonardo, who has previously had a love-affair with the *Novia* whose wedding to the *Novio* is that referred to by the title. The baby to whom the lullaby is addressed is of small significance in the play, and the *Suegra* and *Mujer* are figures peripheral to the main action, which is centred on Leonardo and the *Novia*, but this scene is nevertheless of major importance.

CUADRO SEGUNDO

Habitación pintada de rosa con cobres y ramos de flores populares. En el centro, una mesa con mantel. Es la mañana. Suegra de Leonardo con un niño en brazos. Lo mece. La Mujer, en la otra esquina, hace punto de media.

SUEGRA

Nana, niño, nana
del caballo grande
que no quiso el agua.
El agua era negra
5 dentro de las ramas.
Cuando llega al puente
se detiene y canta.
¿Quién dirá, mi niño,

lo que tiene el agua
10 con su larga cola
por su verde sala?

MUJER (*Bajo*)   Duérmete, clavel,
que el caballo no quiere beber.

SUEGRA   Duérmete, rosal,
15 que el caballo se pone a llorar.
Las patas heridas,
las crines heladas,
dentro de los ojos
un puñal de plata.
20 Bajaban al río.
¡Ay, cómo bajaban!
La sangre corría
mas fuerte que el agua.

MUJER   Duérmete, clavel,
25 que el caballo no quiere beber.

SUEGRA   Duérmete, rosal,
que el caballo se pone a llorar.

MUJER   No quiso tocar
la orilla mojada,
30 su belfo caliente
con moscas de plata.
A los montes duros
solo relinchaba
con el río muerto
35 sobre la garganta.
¡Ay caballo grande
que no quiso el agua!
¡Ay dolor de nieve,
caballo del alba!

SUEGRA	40	¡No vengas! Detente, cierra la ventana con rama de sueños y sueño de ramas.

MUJER   Mi niño se duerme.

SUEGRA   45   Mi niño se calla.

MUJER   Caballo, mi niño
               tiene una almohada.

SUEGRA   Su cuna de acero.

MUJER   Su colcha de holanda.

SUEGRA   50   Nana, niño, nana.

MUJER   ¡Ay caballo grande
               que no quiso el agua!

SUEGRA   ¡No vengas, no entres!
               Vete a la montaña.
           55   Por los valles grises
               donde está la jaca.

MUJER (*Mirando*)   Mi niño se duerme.

SUEGRA   Mi niño descansa.

MUJER (*Bajito*)   Duérmete, clavel,
           60   que el caballo no quiere beber.

SUEGRA (*Levantándose, y muy bajito*)
               Duérmete, rosal,
               que el caballo se pone a llorar.

(*Entran al niño. Entra* LEONARDO) . . .

Traditional elements in this include the *estribillo*; parallelism, with variation of line-ending on the *cosaute* pattern; fluctuation between present and past tenses; exclamation; and the conventionally paired images of the *clavel* and *rosal* (see Part I, Nos. 215 and note, and 217). The main point of these lines is obviously the contrast between, on the one hand, the peace and harmony implicit in the colouring of the setting and in the delivery of the lullaby, and explicit in some of the wording, and, on the other hand, the conflict and disturbance of the negatives *no quiso, ¡no vengas, no entres!*, etc., and the menace of the black water, the wounded horse, the flowing blood, the silver dagger, etc. The horse, throughout the play, is closely linked with Leonardo, who enters immediately after the lullaby, to be questioned by the *Mujer* about the sufferings inflicted on his horse by his frequent and hard riding; later in the scene, after talk of the wedding, hints of Leonardo's involvement with the *Novia*, and his angry departure, the parts of the lullaby referring to blood, the dagger and the wounding are repeated by the weeping *Suegra* and *Mujer*. At the end of this scene, therefore, we are conditioned for the tragedy to come, which is clearly to involve Leonardo.

Lorca's principal source for the horse lullaby is the oral tradition. In his lecture *Las nanas infantiles* he quotes songs from Tamames (Salamanca):

> Las vacas de Juana
> no quieren comer;
> llévalas al agua,
> que querrán beber.

and Pedrosa del Príncipe (Burgos):

> A mi caballo le eché
> hojitas de limón verde,
> y no las quiso comer.

and a lullaby from Granada which is clearly the nucleus of the scene in the play:

> A la nana, nana, nana,
> a la nanita de aquel
> que llevó el caballo al agua
> y lo dejó sin beber.

Lorca's remarks on this lullaby are very relevant to the *nana* scene in the play:

'En esta nana . . . el niño tiene un juego lírico de belleza pura antes de entregarse al sueño. Ese *aquel* y su caballo se alejan por [n.b.] el camino de ramas oscuras hacia el río, para volver a marcharse por donde empieza el canto una vez y otra vez, siempre de manera silenciosa y renovada. Nunca el niño los verá de frente, siempre imaginará en la penumbra el traje oscuro de *aquel* y la grupa brillante del caballo. Ningún personaje de estas canciones da la cara. Es preciso que se alejen y abran un camino hacia sitios donde el agua es más profunda y el pájaro ha renunciado definitivamente a sus alas. Hacia la más simple quietud. Pero la melodía da en este caso un tono que hace dramático en extremo a *aquel* y a su caballo; y al hecho insólito de no darle agua, una rara angustia misteriosa.

En este tipo de canción, el niño reconoce al personaje y, según su experiencia visual, que siempre es más de lo que suponemos, perfila su figura. Está obligado a ser un espectador y un creador al mismo tiempo, ¡y qué creador maravilloso!'

In the lullaby scene of *Bodas de sangre*, the audience or reader is in the position of the child, 'un espectador y un creador al mismo tiempo', but the 'rara angustia misteriosa' is heightened, made more weird and threatening, and the horse, instead of disappearing with the onset of sleep, moves out of the *nana*, to be linked with the lusty and menacing Leonardo in the more mundane dialogue which follows; its hoof beats are to ring through the night and threaten the union of *Novia* and *Novio*, and the silver dagger is to reappear as the instrument of death, the 'cuchillito que apenas cabe en la mano' of the last act.

The complete text of *Bodas de sangre* may be found (as may the early verse collections and the lecture *Las nanas infantiles*) in the edition of Lorca's *Obras completas* published by Aguilar, Madrid. My quotations are from the ninth edition, 1965.

Index of First Lines